AMERICAN THiNK

STUDENT'S BOOK 3

B1+

Herbert Puchta, Jeff Stranks & Peter Lewis-Jones

CAMBRIDGE
UNIVERSITY PRESS

CONTENTS

Contents

Welcome p 4A Music; Verbs of perception; The big screen; Present perfect tenses; TV showsB Our endangered planet; Question tags; So do I / Neither do I; Accepting and refusing invitations; Party time; Indefinite pronouns; Planning a partyC Feeling under the weather; Giving advice; Better or worse?; ComparisonsD Reported speech; Sequencing words; Asking for and offering help; IT problems; IT vocabulary; Passive tenses

	FUNCTIONS & SPEAKING	GRAMMAR	VOCABULARY
Unit 1 Life plans p 12	Talking about the future Complaining	Present tenses (review) Future tenses (review)	Making changes Life plans **WordWise**: Phrases with *up*
Unit 2 Hard times p 20	Talking about the past	Narrative tenses (review) *used to*	Descriptive verbs Time periods
Review Units 1 & 2 pages 28–29			
Unit 3 What's in a name? p 30	Giving advice Expressing obligation Giving recommendations, warnings, and prohibitions	*(don't) have to / ought to / should(n't) / must* *had better (not)* *can('t) / must (not)*	Making and selling Expressions with *name*
Unit 4 Dilemmas p 38	Talking about hypothetical situations Expressing wishes Apologizing and accepting apologies	First and second conditional (review) Time conjunctions *wish* and *if only* Third conditional	Being honest Making a decision **WordWise**: *now*
Review Units 3 & 4 pages 46–47			
Unit 5 What a story! p 48	Telling a story	Relative pronouns Defining and non-defining relative clauses Relative clauses with *which*	Types of stories Elements of a story
Unit 6 How do they do it? p 56	Talking about sequence Explaining how things are done	Present and past passive (review) *have something done* Future and present perfect passive	Extreme adjectives and modifiers *make* and *do*

Pronunciation page 120   **Get it right!** pages 122–124   **Speaking activities** pages 127–128

2

PRONUNCIATION	THINK	SKILLS	
Linking words with *up*	**Train to Think:** Reading between the lines **Self-esteem:** Life changes	Reading Writing Listening	Article: I miss my bad habits Article: For a better life … Photostory: What's up with Mia? An email about resolutions A conversation about famous people who started their careers late
Initial consonant clusters with /s/	**Train to Think:** Following an idea through a paragraph **Values:** Animal rights	Reading Writing Listening	Article: The great fire of London Article: Family life in 17th-century Britain Culture: Where life is really hard A magazine article about a historic event A class presentation about animals being put on trial
Strong and weak forms: /ɑv/ and /əv/	**Train to Think:** Identifying the main topic of a paragraph **Self-esteem:** People and their names	Reading Writing Listening	Article: Brand names Article: Crazy names Fiction: *Wild Country* by Margaret Johnson A reply to a letter asking for advice A conversation about techniques for remembering names
Consonant–vowel word linking	**Train to Think:** Thinking of consequences **Values:** Doing the right thing	Reading Writing Listening	Quiz: What would YOU do? Article: The day Billy Ray's life changed forever Photostory: And the hole gets deeper! A diary entry about a dilemma A guessing game: Famous Wishes
/ə/ in word endings	**Train to Think:** Thinking about different writing styles **Self-esteem:** A better world	Reading Writing Listening	Article: Everybody loves stories – but why? Article: Hollywood fairy tales Culture: Ireland: A nation of storytellers A fairy tale A conversation about a short story
The /ʒ/ phoneme	**Train to Think:** Understanding what's relevant **Self-esteem:** Life changes	Reading Writing Listening	Article: The man who walks on air Blog: How Do They Do That? Fiction: *The Mind Map* by David Morrison Explaining how things are done A conversation about a new tattoo

WELCOME

A THAT'S ENTERTAINMENT!
Music

1 🔊 1.02 **Complete the conversation with the words. Then listen and check.**

~~looking~~ | can't | makes | talent show | mad
songs | look | feel | sound | guitar | get

LISA   Hey, Kim, what are you ⁰ _looking_ at?

KIM   My science book. Can't you see I'm busy?

LISA   I'm just asking. Sorry.

KIM   No, I'm sorry. I don't ¹_____ great today.

LISA   You don't ²_____ very happy. What's the matter?

KIM   My dad ³_____ me so ⁴_____.

LISA   That doesn't ⁵_____ good. Why?

KIM   He says I ⁶_____ be in the band.

LISA   What?! So you can't play in the ⁷_____ next week?

KIM   No. He says no music until after final exams.

LISA   But finals aren't over for four weeks!

KIM   I know. He wants me to study and forget about writing ⁸_____. I can't even practice the ⁹_____.

LISA   But you need some time to relax.

KIM   I know. I ¹⁰_____ so angry when I think about it. It just isn't fair.

2 🔊 1.02 **Listen again. Answer the questions.**

1   Why is Kim angry?
2   How long is it until her exams are over?
3   What does Lisa think about the situation?
4   Who do you agree with: Kim or her dad? Why?

3 **SPEAKING** **What do your parents allow you to do during exam time? What don't they let you do? Make lists. Then compare with a partner.**

4 **In your notebook, sort the words into two categories. Label the categories. Then think of four more items for each one.**

drums | classical | jazz | violin
guitar | pop | piano | rap

Verbs of perception

1 **Complete the sentences from the conversation with the correct forms of (not) look. Then match them with the rules.**

1   You _____ very happy.
2   Hey, Kim, what _____ at?

> **RULE:** We use verbs of perception (*look, smell, feel, taste*) …
>
> in the present continuous to talk about actions. ☐
>
> in the simple present to talk about states. ☐

2 **Complete the mini-dialogues with the correct forms of the verbs.**

1   taste
   A   What are you doing?
   B   I _____ the soup. It _____ great.
2   smell
   A   My socks _____ really bad!
   B   Then why _____ you _____ them?
3   feel
   A   Why _____ you _____ that sweater?
   B   Because it's so soft. I like the way it _____.

3 **Work in pairs. Kim tries to persuade her dad to let her play in the talent show. Write a conversation of eight lines. Then read it out.**

The big screen

1 **SPEAKING** Work in pairs. For each type of movie, think of an example that you have both seen.

action | animated | comedy | drama | horror | romantic comedy | science fiction | thriller

2 Read the article. What types of movies does it mention?

3 Read the article again and mark the sentences T (true), F (false), or DS (doesn't say).

1 Chris Columbus's movies are popular with kids 13–18 years old. ☐

2 Columbus started making movies when he was 30. ☐

3 His movies aren't popular with older people. ☐

4 Lots of people in Hollywood want Columbus to make movies. ☐

5 He's never won an Oscar. ☐

4 **SPEAKING** Work in pairs. Think of your favorite movie director and discuss these questions.

1 What movies has this director made?

2 What do you like about his/her movies?

Present perfect tenses

Complete the sentences. Use the present perfect or present perfect continuous form of the verbs and ⟨circle⟩ the correct words.

1 They _____ (play) *for / since* 87 minutes, and neither team has scored yet.

2 I _____ (not watch) the last episode *already / yet*, so don't say which singer won.

3 _____ you _____ (see) last night's show *already / yet*? Brad Pitt and Lady Gaga were guests.

4 The children _____ (sit) in front of the TV watching cartoons *for / since* they got up.

5 It's the funniest show on TV. I _____ (not miss) an episode *already / yet*.

6 The president _____ (say) the same thing *for / since* weeks now. No one believes him.

Behind the camera

Chris Columbus

A 12-year-old who gets left behind when his family goes on vacation, a teenage magician fighting to save his world, and the troubled son of a Greek god living in modern-day America: these are just three of the characters brought to life on the big screen by director Chris Columbus. With movies such as *Home Alone*, *Harry Potter and the Chamber of Secrets*, and *Percy Jackson and the Sea of Monsters*, Columbus has certainly shown that he knows how to get teenagers into the theaters.

Columbus has been making movies for more than 30 years and has become one of the most successful movie directors of all time. Since he directed his first movie, *Adventures in Babysitting*, in 1987, Columbus has been involved in some of the biggest movies as both a director and a producer.

But Columbus doesn't only make action movies for the teenage market. He's also made a number of successful movies for adults. Comedies such as *Mrs. Doubtfire*, dramas such as *The Help*, and science fiction movies such as *Bicentennial Man* have all helped make Columbus one of Hollywood's most popular filmmakers.

TV shows

1 Work in pairs. Look at the sentences in the previous exercise. Match them with the types of TV show.

talent show ☐ | sitcom ☐ | cartoon ☐ | sports program ☐ | the news ☐ | talk show ☐

2 Choose a type of TV show from the list below. Write a sentence about it using the present perfect and/or present perfect continuous. Don't include the type of show in your sentence!

drama series | game show | reality show | soap (opera)

I've been watching it for weeks, but no one has won the million-dollar prize yet.

3 **SPEAKING** Read your sentence aloud. Can the rest of the class guess the type of TV show?

B TIME TO ACT
Our endangered planet

1 **SPEAKING** Work in pairs. Describe the photos. What problems do they show?

2 🔊 1.03 Listen to three conversations. Match them with the photos.

3 🔊 1.03 Listen again. In which conversation do you hear these words? Write the number.

a trash ☐   c litter ☐   e fumes ☐   g flooding ☐
b global warming ☐   d pollution ☐   f smog ☐

Question tags

1 Complete these sentences from the recording with the question tags.

are they? | aren't they? | does it?
did they? | is it? | isn't it?
weren't they? | doesn't it?

1 I guess they're just lazy, _____
2 But it only takes a few people to spoil everything, _____
3 Yes, it's all those fumes from the factory, _____
4 They didn't ask us if we wanted it here, _____
5 Even if they do, it doesn't make our lives any better, _____
6 Hundreds of homes were damaged, _____
7 And the politicians aren't really doing anything to help, _____
8 It isn't the sort of thing you expect to see here, _____

2 Complete the sentences with question tags.

1 You haven't told Ron, _____?
2 You're going to do something about it, _____?
3 It sounds really dangerous, _____?
4 It didn't work, _____?
5 It won't be easy, _____?
6 She wrote an angry letter to the town council, _____?

So do I / Neither do I

1 Look at the questions and complete the answers with *so* or *neither*.

1 A I don't really believe in that stuff.
   B _____ do I.

2 A I think we should do something.
   B _____ do I.

2 **SPEAKING** Complete the sentences so that they are true for you. Agree (or disagree!) with your partner's sentences.

1 I really like …
2 I don't like …
3 I believe …
4 I don't believe …

Accepting and refusing invitations

1 🔊 1.04 Put the sentences in order to make a conversation. Then listen and check.

1	a SUE	Marco and I want to do something to help the flood victims.
☐	b SUE	Yes – 20 kilometers! <u>Want to join us?</u>
☐	c SUE	<u>That's a shame.</u> But <u>you will</u> make a pledge, <u>won't you?</u>
☐	d SUE	We're going to do a charity walk on Sunday.
☐	e DEREK	<u>Of course I will.</u>
☐	f DEREK	Are you going to walk a long way?
☐	g DEREK	What are you going to do?
☐	h DEREK	<u>I'd love to, but I can't.</u> I'm busy.

2 Work in pairs. Write a conversation using the <u>underlined</u> phrases from Exercise 1.

You and your friend are tired of all the litter in the street and have decided to do something about it. What are you going to do? Invite another friend to join you.

Party time

1 Work in pairs. Imagine you're planning a party. Make a list of important things to do.

2 Read the article. Does it mention the things on your list?

How to plan a party

The first question you need to ask is, "Why am I having a party?" (It's my birthday; finals are over; our soccer team won a game; I just want a party.)

All the best parties have a theme. What are you going to choose for yours? Beach party? 1970s disco? Something else? You also need to find
1_____ to hold your party. Wherever you decide to have it, it's probably a good idea to
2_____ permission from your parents first.

Next, who are you going to invite: 3_____ you know or just some of your friends? It's time to
4_____ a guest list. Remember: Think carefully about how many people you can afford to invite. When your list is ready, you can
5_____ the invitations. Two weeks before the party is the best time. Any sooner, and people might forget about the party; any later, and some of your guests might already have other plans.

OK, so now you've got two weeks to get it all ready. Don't panic – it's plenty of time, but don't leave
6_____ until the last minute. If you want to
7_____ a DJ, start looking now. Remember that he or she might want you to 8_____ a deposit, so make sure you have the money for that. Then you need to 9_____ for the food and
10_____ the room, although these things can be left until the day before.

Finally, get a good night's sleep the night before, give yourself a few hours to get the last few things ready, and then, most importantly, have fun!

3 Read the article again and complete it with the missing words.

get | send out | arrange | pay
everyone | hire | decorate
somewhere | make | everything

Indefinite pronouns

1 🔊 1.05 Complete the conversation with suitable indefinite pronouns (everyone, somewhere, nothing, etc.). Then listen and check.

TOM Is ¹_____ ready for the party?
JADE No, ²_____ is ready. We haven't found ³_____ to have it, even. We've looked ⁴_____.
TOM Have you invited ⁵_____ yet?
JADE Yes, we've invited 50 people, and ⁶_____ is coming!
TOM So, you have 50 people coming but ⁷_____ for them to hang out?
JADE That's right.
TOM Well, we have to do ⁸_____. How about using my house?
JADE What about your parents?
TOM They won't mind. They're going away ⁹_____ for the weekend. I'll make sure ¹⁰_____ is cleaned up before they get home.

2 Read the next part of the story and continue the conversation. Write four more lines. Use at least one indefinite pronoun.

It's the day after the party. Tom's mom and dad arrive home and open the door…

MOM What is this? Look at our house!
DAD Tom! TOM!
TOM Oh, hi, Mom. Hi, Dad. You're home early. Did you have a good time?

Planning a party

SPEAKING Work in pairs to plan a party. Be creative! Think about:

- what it's for
- the theme
- who to invite
- where it will be
- food and drink
- music

C IN MY OPINION, …
Feeling under the weather

1 🔊 1.06 **Listen to the conversation. What's the matter with Jen?**

2 Complete the conversation with the words.

appointment | should | operation
energy | ought to | get
physically | exercised

MOM You don't look well, Jen. What's up?

JEN I'm just tired all the time, Mom. You know, I don't have any
¹_____.

MOM Are you sleeping OK?

JEN Not great, no. I often wake up in the night.

MOM Well, you know, Jen, you ²_____ exercise more. That would help.

JEN Really?

MOM Yes. I mean, if you ³_____ more, you'd be more tired ⁴_____, and then you'd sleep better.

JEN You're joking, right? I run, I go swimming, I go for long walks. My problem isn't exercise.

MOM Well, that's true. Maybe you ⁵_____ see a doctor. I can call and make an ⁶_____ for you, if you want.

JEN A doctor? I don't think so. I don't feel sick – just tired. I'm sure I'll ⁷_____ better soon.

MOM OK, well, we can talk about it later. I'm going out to see a friend of mine who had an ⁸_____ last week.

JEN OK, Mom. Hope your friend's all right. And don't worry about me. I'll be fine.

3 Match the verbs 1–6 with a–f to make phrases. Sometimes there's more than one possible combination.

1	feel	a	an appointment
2	get	b	an operation
3	have	c	a doctor
4	make	d	better
5	see	e	sick

4 Write down as many words related to health as you can think of. Then compare with a partner.

sick, nurse, hospital, …

Giving advice

1 Complete the sentences with *should(n't)* or *ought to*.

1 It's late. You _____ go.

2 If you aren't well, you _____ see a doctor.

3 Jane's in the hospital. We _____ go and visit her.

4 The doctor is very busy, so you _____ make an appointment. Don't just show up.

5 Your knee hurts? Well, you _____ play soccer today, then.

6 If you want to get better, you _____ rest as much as possible.

2 Match the problems 1–3 with the pieces of advice a–c. Then write one more piece of advice for each problem. Use *should(n't)* and *ought to*.

1 My hand really hurts. ☐

2 I think I'm going to be late for school. ☐

3 I can't do this homework. ☐

a You ought to hurry.

b Maybe you should call a friend.

c You ought to see a doctor.

3 SPEAKING Work in pairs. Write mini-dialogues that include the problems and advice in Exercise 2. Add two or three lines to each. Then act them out.

Why all these awards?

I'm really tired of awards ceremonies and prizes. Why do we have to compare things? Everywhere you look, there's someone talking about who or what is "the best" or "the most comfortable" or "the biggest," and so on. And sometimes the prize winners aren't the best anyway!

Here's an example: the Oscars in 2014. I saw the movie *Gravity*, and it was the most exciting movie I'd ever seen. But did it win the Oscar for Best Picture? No! They gave the award to *Twelve Years A Slave*! Can you believe it? It wasn't as good as *Gravity* at all.

OK, *Gravity* was the most successful movie at the Oscars – it got seven awards – but I don't think that's enough. Sandra Bullock was fantastic as Dr. Ryan.

I think she's much better than Cate Blanchett, who won Best Actress. But the good thing is that *Gravity* won Best Visual Effects – I've never seen anything as fantastic. And was the music good? It was great! No other movie had music as fantastic as that.

I said all these things to my friend Dave the day after the Oscars. I told him I thought the judges were the craziest people in the world. Dave asked me how many movies I'd seen in 2013. I said, "One – *Gravity*." Dave says he doesn't know anyone as stupid as me.

Better or worse?

1 Read the blog entry. Mark the sentences T (true) or F (false).

1 The writer likes awards ceremonies. ☐
2 *Gravity* won Best Picture at the 2014 Oscars. ☐
3 The writer thinks the visual effects in *Gravity* are the best he's ever seen. ☐
4 Dave thinks the writer is very intelligent. ☐

2 SPEAKING Work in pairs. Discuss these questions.

1 What other awards ceremonies do you know of?
2 Do you like awards ceremonies? Why (not)?
3 Do you think it's fair to compare different movies, actors, music, etc., and choose one as the best?

Comparisons

1 Complete the sentences with the correct form of the adjectives and adverbs. Add any other necessary words.

1 The weather tomorrow won't be _____ (cold) as today.
2 This is the _____ (good) pizza I've ever eaten.
3 Do you think this is _____ (difficult) than the other test?
4 This book's OK, but it isn't the _____ (interesting) one I've ever read.
5 She learns things _____ (easy) than I do.
6 I'm not very good at tennis, but I'm _____ (not bad) as Janice!
7 Hurry up! Can't you walk _____ (quick) than that?

2 SPEAKING Work in pairs or small groups. Discuss these statements. Do you agree or disagree with them? Why?

1 The best things in life are free.
2 If something is more expensive, it's always better.
3 It's more important to work hard than to play hard.
4 Exercise isn't as important as good sleep.

3 Choose two things or people from one of these categories. Write a paragraph comparing them.

sports that you like | actors that you like
towns or cities that you know | school subjects
books that you have read

D HELP!
Reported speech

1 Read the story and answer the questions.

1 What had happened to the caller's computer screen?
2 What three things did Graham ask the caller to do?
3 Why couldn't the caller turn on the lights?
4 What did Graham finally say to the caller?
5 What happened to Graham in the end?

We asked readers to tell us about a time when they tried to help someone. Here's one from Graham Smith.

I used to work in IT for a big company, but I was fired because I got angry with a manager. Here's what happened.

I answered the phone one day and said, "Hi. Can I help you?" A voice said, "Hi. I'm a manager in the Sales Department, and I've got an IT problem. I need your help." "What's the problem?" I asked, and he told me his computer screen had suddenly gone black.

¹_____, I couldn't think why it had happened. I asked him to check that the screen was still connected. He said it was. ²_____ I asked him if he'd pressed any buttons by mistake. He said, "No, the computer was installing a program when, suddenly, it went 'poof'!"

³_____ a few seconds, I said, "OK, please check that your computer is still plugged into the wall. Sometimes it gets disconnected accidentally." The manager asked me to wait a minute. Then he came back and said, "I can't see behind my desk where the plug is. It's very dark." So I told him to turn the light on. Do you know what he said? "Oh, I can't turn the light on because the electricity went out five minutes ago."

I tried to keep quiet. ⁴_____, I had to say something. I warned him never to call me again, ever. He complained to my boss, and I was fired. How fair is that, do you think?

2 Rewrite the sentences in reported speech.

0 "I need your help."
He said that _____*he needed my help.*_____

1 "What's the problem?"
I asked him _____

2 "I can't see because it's very dark."
He said that _____

3 "Please check that your computer is still plugged in."
I asked him to _____

4 "I can't turn the light on because the electricity went out five minutes ago."
He said that _____

Sequencing words

Match these words with spaces 1–4 in the story.

a After ☐   c Finally ☐
b Then ☐   d At first ☐

Asking for and offering help

1 Put the words in order to make questions.

1 I / you / Can / help / ?   ☐
_____

2 help / that / you / I / Can / with / ?   ☐
_____

3 me / you / Could / a / lend / hand / ?   ☐
_____

4 you / Do / help / any / need / ?   ☐
_____

5 you / minutes / Do / a / have / few / ?   ☐
_____

2 Look at the sentences in Exercise 1 again. Mark them A (asking for help) or O (offering help).

3 SPEAKING Work in pairs. Choose a situation and write a conversation in which A asks B for help. Use expressions from Exercise 1. Then act it out.

IT problems

1 **SPEAKING** Work in pairs. What do the pictures show?

A ☐

B ☐

C ☐

2 🔊 1.07 Listen to three conversations. Match them with the pictures in Exercise 1.

3 🔊 1.07 Listen again. In which conversation do you hear these words? Write the number.

a attachment ☐   e install ☐
b coverage ☐   f online ☐
c downloaded ☐   g program ☐
d file ☐   h upload ☐

IT vocabulary

1 Circle the correct words.

1 *go / have* online
2 *send / install* a message
3 *file / type* your password
4 *install / go* a program
5 *attach / activate* a file
6 *download / go* a file
7 *upload / type* a photo
8 *go / delete* a message
9 *open / install* an attachment
10 *post / buy* an app
11 *upload / turn on* airplane mode
12 *have / go* network coverage

2 Match the verbs with the nouns. Make as many combinations as you can.

a message | a photo | airplane mode | a password
an attachment | a program | a file | an app

0 install _____ *a program / an app*
1 attach _____
2 download _____
3 upload _____
4 open _____
5 post _____
6 delete _____
7 turn on _____
8 type _____

Passive tenses

1 Complete the sentences from the conversations with the verb forms.

is being repaired | was taken | is installed

1 The photo _____ on a safari trip.
2 Just click on it, and the program _____ automatically.
3 The network _____ out here.

2 Rewrite the sentences in the passive.

0 Someone posted a message.
  A message was posted.
1 Someone is downloading a program.
  _____
2 Someone has installed a new program.
  _____
3 Someone has typed the password.
  _____
4 Someone is repairing the hard drive.
  _____
5 Someone deleted the message.
  _____

3 Describe one of these processes using the passive.
  • downloading an app to your phone
  • uploading a photo to a social networking site

1 | LIFE PLANS

READING

1 What are the people doing in the photos? Do you think these are good or bad habits? Why?

2 Check (✓) the bad habits that you have. Then add two more of your own.

☐ not getting enough exercise

☐ leaving your homework until the last minute

☐ forgetting important dates

☐ texting when you shouldn't

☐ playing computer games when you should be studying

☐ getting up late for school

3 **SPEAKING** Work in pairs. What can you do to change some of these habits?

4 Read the article quickly. Underline the two things that the writer is trying to change about her life.

5 ◀))1.08 Read the article again and listen. Mark the sentences T (true) or F (false).

1 The writer has to finish the article by the following day. ☐

2 The writer is finding it easy to lead a healthier life. ☐

3 We use different parts of our brain depending on who we're thinking about. ☐

4 Our brains don't always let us make good choices for our future selves. ☐

5 It takes just under two months for our brains to adjust to changes in our lifestyles. ☐

6 The writer has decided that she'll never be able to change her habits. ☐

I miss my bad habits

I don't believe it! It's 11 p.m., and I'm still sitting here writing this article for the school magazine! I've had two weeks to write it, and my teacher wants it tomorrow. She's always complaining that I leave things till the last minute. Maybe she's right.

A month ago I made a resolution to be more efficient this year. Well, I've clearly failed that one. I've also been trying to get fitter for four weeks now. I've started going to the gym, I've taken up karate, and I've changed my diet. I've even been going to bed earlier. But I'm not feeling any fitter, just a little unhappier.

Right now, I guess kids all over the country are thinking back to the resolutions they made at the beginning of the school year. Some of them have already given up for this year. Others are still doing well. Many, I suspect, like me, are struggling with them. I miss my bad habits. Why is leading a better life so hard?

I've just read an article on a website, and I've discovered that it isn't my fault! In fact, it isn't anyone's fault. It's our brains. They're programmed to make it difficult to break bad habits.

There's nothing we can do. For example, you're sitting up late playing Minecraft. You know you have an important test tomorrow, so why don't you just turn off the computer and go to bed? Scientists have done experiments that show we use one part of our brain when we think about ourselves and another when we think about other people. However, when we think about ourselves in the future, we use the same part of the brain that we usually use to think about other people. In other words, the brain sees the "future you" as a different person than your "present you." And that's why we don't always find it easy to make sensible decisions for ourselves in the future.

But that's not all. Scientists have also discovered that it takes around ten weeks to form a good habit. For example, it's going to take another six weeks before going to the gym stops being so difficult and becomes an automatic part of my life. That's the amount of time the brain needs to accept new behavioral patterns. The good news is that once you make it to ten weeks, everything becomes a lot easier. The bad news is that ten weeks is a really long time, so it's easy to give up on your good intentions before then.

So even when we want to change our ways and become better people, our brains won't let us. Or is this just an excuse? Look – I've finished my article on time! Anything is possible!

▌▌TRAIN TO THiNK ▌▌▌▌

Reading between the lines

Sometimes a writer doesn't tell us everything directly. We need to draw conclusions from the information the writer gives. We call this "reading between the lines."

6 Answer the questions and give reasons for your answers.

  0 Who is the writer? (paragraph 1)
    She's a student — she's writing for the school magazine and mentions her teacher.

  1 Does the writer feel guilty that she hasn't finished the article? (paragraph 1)

  2 Does she enjoy exercise? (paragraph 2)

SPEAKING

Work in pairs. Discuss these questions.

1 What resolutions are you going to make for this school year?

2 What do you think is the secret to changing your life for the better?

Careful planning.

Do work first, play later.

Listen to your parents.

GRAMMAR
Present tenses (review)

1 **Match sentences 1–5 with the tenses a–d and then complete the rule with the tenses (a–d).**

1 **I'm** still **sitting** here writing this article. ☐

2 I've also **been trying** to get fitter for four weeks now. ☐

3 **I've started** going to the gym. ☐

4 **I'm not feeling** any fitter, just a little unhappier. ☐

5 The brain **sees** the "future you" as a different person to your "present you." ☐

a present perfect continuous

b simple present

c present continuous (x2)

d present perfect

RULE:

1 We use the _____ to talk about facts and give opinions.

2 We use the _____ to talk about what's happening at or around the time of speaking.

3 We use the _____ to talk about past actions without saying when they happened.

4 We use the _____ to talk about actions that started in the past and are still happening.

> **LOOK!** We can use the present continuous with *always* to complain about behavior that we don't like and find annoying.
> *My dad's always telling me what to do.*

2 **Complete the text with the correct present tense form of the verbs. Sometimes more than one tense is possible.**

It's 2 a.m., and I ¹_____ (lie) in bed. I ²_____ (try) to get to sleep, but I can't. I ³_____ (have) trouble sleeping for about a month now. I ⁴_____ (try) different things to help me sleep, but nothing ⁵_____ (work). My mind ⁶_____ (not want) to stop. A lot ⁷_____ (happen) in my life right now. It's exam time, so I ⁸_____ (study) a lot. There's also the question of next year. I ⁹_____ (think) about it for ages. Mom and Dad ¹⁰_____ (want) me to go to college, but I'm just not sure what to do.

3 **SPEAKING** **Work in pairs. Think about a problem you've been having, and tell your partner.**

> *I've been fighting a lot with my little brother recently. I've tried to ignore him, but it's impossible.*

Workbook page 10 ➤

VOCABULARY
Making changes

1 **Match the phrases with the definitions.**

0 quit doing something — *a*

1 make a resolution ☐

2 do well ☐

3 struggle with something ☐

4 take something up ☐

5 break a bad habit ☐

6 form a good habit ☐

7 change your ways ☐

a stop doing something

b find something difficult

c start a new hobby or interest

d stop doing something that isn't good for you

e start doing something that is good for you

f decide to make a positive change

g do things differently (usually for the better)

h be successful

2 **Complete the text with the missing verbs.**

⊝ ☐ ☒　　　◀ ▶ ⌂

Last year I ¹_____ lots of resolutions and decided to ²_____ my ways. I tried to ³_____ the habit of getting up late on weekends. For two months I got up at 8 a.m. But by 2 p.m. I felt sleepy, so I ⁴_____ up sleeping in the afternoon. I also ⁵_____ wasting time online, but my parents bought me a laptop, and that was the end of that. Then I stopped eating meat. I was ⁶_____ well until Mom made roast beef. I just had to eat it. I tried to ⁷_____ good habits as well: for example, I started piano lessons. But I ⁸_____ with finding time to practice, so I stopped. This year I've only made one resolution: not to make any resolutions.

3 **SPEAKING** **Work in pairs. Discuss these questions.**

1 What subjects are you doing well in at school?

2 What subjects do you struggle with?

3 What was the last thing you quit doing? Why?

Workbook page 12 ➤

LISTENING

J.K. Rowling

Sylvester Stallone

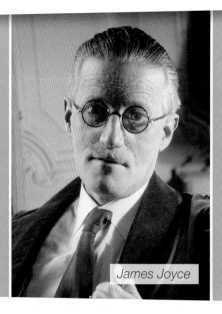

James Joyce

1 **SPEAKING** Work in pairs. Discuss these questions.

1 What do you know about these people?
2 Can you match the information with each person?

A _____ was a famous Irish writer.

B _____ wrote *Rocky*.

C _____ wrote the Harry Potter series.

2 🔊 1.09 Listen and check.

3 🔊 1.09 Read the questions carefully. Listen again and make notes.

1 What's Annie's problem?
2 What does Ben want to do with his life?
3 How was James Joyce earning a living when he was 30?
4 How are the examples of Joyce, Stallone, and Rowling different from Annie's situation?
5 Why does Ben tell Annie not to worry?

4 **SPEAKING** Work in pairs. Compare your answers to Exercise 3.

GRAMMAR
Future tenses (review)

1 Look at the sentences from the listening. Complete them with the correct future forms of the verbs. Then complete the rule with *present continuous*, *going to*, and *will*.

1 I _____ (meet) the career advisor this afternoon.

2 I _____ (study) medicine.

3 I'm sure you _____ (do) well whatever you do.

> **RULE:**
>
> • To talk about future plans, we often use the
> 1 _____ .
>
> • To make predictions, we often use
> 2 _____ .
>
> • To talk about intentions, we often use
> 3 _____ .

2 (Circle) the best tense.

1 *We'll go* / *We're going* to the beach this Friday. Do you want to come?
2 I don't think *I'll finish* / *I'm finishing* this homework.
3 *I won't go* / *I'm not going* to college this year. I want to take a year off.
4 I have a dentist appointment tomorrow. *I'm seeing* / *I'll see* her at 10 a.m.
5 Daisy's learning to fly. *She'll be* / *She's going to be* a pilot.
6 I'm not *eating* / *going to eat* chocolate. That's my resolution for next year.
7 Argentina *will win* / *are winning* the next World Cup. That's what I think.
8 *We're flying* / *We will fly* on Friday. I'm so excited.

3 In your notebook, write down:

1 two plans you have for this week.
2 two intentions you have for this year.
3 two predictions for your life.

Workbook page 11 ▶

READING

1 **SPEAKING** Check (✓) the statements you agree with. Then discuss them in pairs.

A good friend …

☐ always tells you what they're thinking.
☐ never criticizes you.
☐ agrees with everything you say.
☐ always listens when you have a problem.

2 Read the article. Decide which paragraph each of these headings describes and write them in the correct places.

No one is happy all the time

Stop expecting everybody to like you

Don't expect people to always agree with you

Stop expecting people to know what you're thinking

Don't expect people to change

3 Read the article again. Which paragraphs should these people read and think about? There may be more than one possible answer.

1 "Billy's so unfriendly to me. I don't know what I've done wrong."
2 "Can't they see I don't really feel like talking? I just want them to leave me alone."
3 "Katie always has a smile on her face. I wish my life was as perfect as hers."
4 "I think Jenny would be a great drummer for our band. I don't know what your problem is."
5 "I wish Dylan wasn't so sloppy. He always makes such a mess."

4 **SPEAKING** Work in pairs. Discuss these questions.

1 Which piece of advice do you think is the best? Why?
2 What other advice would you add?

For a better life ...

Life can be hard, and when our plans don't work out, it's often easy to blame others. Sometimes we expect too much from friends and family, and when they don't act as we think they should, we feel disappointed. Maybe it would be easier if we stopped expecting so much from other people. No one is perfect, and that includes you.

1 _____

So you want to travel the world before you get your degree, but your parents don't think it's a good idea. Of course, it's great if other people can support you in your decisions, but you can't keep everyone happy all of the time. It's your life, and you need to make the decisions to make you happy.

2 _____

Don't worry if there are people who aren't very nice to you because there are plenty of people who are. They're called your friends. Spend time with them and avoid the others. And when it comes to finding that special person and settling down, remember: There's somebody for everyone.

3 _____

You've been practicing soccer all summer. You think you're good enough to be on the school team, but the coach doesn't seem to be thinking the same thing. Maybe he just hasn't thought about it at all. He isn't a mind reader, so tell him. Then at least he knows what you're thinking. He might even choose you.

4 _____

People can change, but they don't usually do it because someone else wants them to. You can try to tell them what you're not so happy about, so at least they know, but don't be too disappointed if they continue doing exactly the same things. You have a choice: Accept them or walk away.

5 _____

From their Facebook updates, you'd believe that all your friends are happy all the time and leading exciting lives. Of course, they aren't, just like you know that your life isn't always perfect. We all go through hard times, and we often try to hide it. Be kind to people. They might be having a bad day, and your smile could make a big difference.

VOCABULARY
Life plans

1 Match the phrases with the pictures.
Write 1–8 in the boxes.

1	retire	5	start a family
2	travel the world	6	settle down
3	start a career	7	get promoted
4	get a degree	8	leave school

2 Complete the text with phrases from Exercise 1.
Use the correct forms of the verbs.

My uncle is so cool. He ¹_____ when he was 16 because he wanted to see other places. He spent the next 20 years ²_____, working in restaurants and hotels in many different countries. When he was in his early forties, he decided to return to the U.S. He went to college and ³_____. He did really well, and when he finished, he ⁴_____ as a translator. Because he was good at his job, he ⁵_____ quickly. Soon he was Head Translator. When he was 48, he met the love of his life, and they decided to ⁶_____ and ⁷_____. Now he's 55, with three young children. He says he wants ⁸_____ soon. He wants to stop working and take the whole family around the world with him.

Workbook page 12 ▶

THiNK SELF-ESTEEM

Life changes

1 Complete the table with your own ideas.

	One positive change	One negative change
You leave home.	*Freedom*	*You have to take care of yourself.*
You get a degree.		
You start a career.		
You start a family.		
You get promoted.		
You retire.		

2 **SPEAKING** Work in small groups. Compare your ideas.

WRITING
An email about resolutions

Write an email to an English-speaking friend in another country. Describe your resolutions for the coming school year. Write about:

• bad habits you're changing   • new classes you're taking   • a hobby you plan to take up   • why you're doing all of this

What's up with Mia?

1 **Look at the photos and answer the questions.**

What do you think the problem is?
What does Mia want to give up?

2 🔊 **1.10** **Now read and listen to the photostory. Check your answers.**

FLORA Hi, Leo. Hi, Jeff.
LEO Hi, Flora.
FLORA Hey, has either of you seen Mia lately?
JEFF No. I haven't seen her for a while, actually.
LEO Now that you mention it, neither have I.
FLORA It's strange, isn't it? She hasn't been to the café in a long time. I wonder what she's up to.
LEO Hey, look who it is. Hi, Mia! We were just talking about you. Where have you been hiding?

MIA Don't even joke about it. I never have time to do anything anymore.
FLORA Come and sit down. I'll get you something to drink.
MIA You're the best. Thank you so much.
JEFF So, what's up, Mia? Why are you so busy?
MIA Where do I start? Mondays, I'm taking a French class after school. Tuesdays, I have tennis lessons. Wednesdays, it's swimming. Thursdays, I have orchestra. And every night I'm up late doing homework.
LEO It's Thursday today.
MIA I know. I'm only here because orchestra was canceled this week. Thank goodness.
LEO Don't you like playing the violin?
MIA Not really. I mean, I like playing an instrument. I just don't think I want to continue with the violin. Do you realize I spend up to an hour every day practicing?
FLORA So, why do you do it?
MIA To make my mom happy, I guess.
JEFF You should talk to her. Tell her you want to quit the violin.
MIA Yeah, maybe. But it's not always so easy to talk to her.
FLORA Well, you need to do something. You don't have any time for yourself. I mean, we never get to hang out with you anymore.
MIA Yeah, I guess you're right. It's up to me to do something about this.

THE FOLLOWING WEEK ...

CHLOE Hi, Mia.
MIA Hi, Chloe.
CHLOE What's up with you? You don't sound very happy.
MIA It's nothing.
CHLOE Really?
MIA Well, to be honest, I don't really feel like orchestra today.
CHLOE Why not?
MIA I haven't had any time to practice. And I'm tired. I'm just not up for it.
CHLOE Don't be silly. I'm sure it'll be fine. Look, Mr. Wales wants to start. Come on, Mia.
MIA Here we go. I am *not* looking forward to this.

DEVELOPING SPEAKING

3 Work in pairs. Discuss what you think Mia decides to do. Write down your ideas.

We think that Mia decides to keep playing the violin in the orchestra.

4 ◀ EP1 Watch and find out how the story continues.

5 Answer the questions.

1 What happens at orchestra practice?
2 What reasons does Mia give her mom for giving up the violin?
3 Why does Mia think her mom changed her mind?
4 How is Mia learning the guitar?
5 Why does Mia enjoy playing the guitar?

PHRASES FOR FLUENCY

1 Find these expressions in the photostory. Who says them? How do you say them in your language?

1 Now that you mention it, … _____
2 Where have you been hiding? _____
3 You're the best. _____
4 Where do I start? _____
5 Don't be silly. _____
6 Here we go. _____

2 Use the expressions in Exercise 1 to complete the conversations.

1 A You look tired. Have you had a busy day?
   B Busy? _____ First, I had a math test. Then I had a drama club meeting at lunchtime. Then we had to run in gym class …
   A Well, you just sit down, and I'll get you something to eat.
   B Thanks, Mom. _____

2 A _____, Annie? I haven't seen you for days.
   B I haven't been anywhere. You're the one who's disappeared.
   A _____, I've just been really busy lately, that's all.

3 A It's ten o'clock. Time for the test.
   B _____ I'm really not ready for this.
   A Me neither. I have a feeling I'm not going to pass.
   B _____ You always pass.

WordWise
Phrases with *up*

1 Match the phrases in bold with the definitions.

1 So **what's up**, Mia? ☐
2 I spend **up to** an hour a day practicing. ☐
3 I wonder what she's **up to**. ☐
4 Every night I'm **up late** doing homework. ☐
5 It's **up to me** to do something about this. ☐
6 I'm just not **up for** it. ☐

a still awake
b doing
c what's happening?
d excited about
e as long as / to a maximum of
f my responsibility

2 Use words and phrases from Exercise 1 to complete the sentences.

1 What have you been _____ recently?
2 I was _____ watching TV last night.
3 Oh, no! You look really unhappy. _____?
4 It isn't my decision. It's _____ you to decide.
5 My head hurts. I'm not _____ a rock concert.
6 This car can carry _____ six people.

Workbook page 12

Pronunciation
Linking words with *up*
Go to page 120.   🔊

FUNCTIONS
Complaining

1 Match the parts of the sentences.

1 I'm not happy with ☐   a it takes up so much time.
2 The problem is that ☐
3 He's always ☐   b picking on me.
4 To be honest, I don't ☐   c really like the violin.
   d the way he talks to me.

2 ROLE PLAY Work in pairs. Student A: Go to page 127. Student B: Go to page 128.

2 HARD TIMES

OBJECTIVES

FUNCTIONS: talking about the past
GRAMMAR: narrative tenses (review); *used to*
VOCABULARY: descriptive verbs; time periods

READING

1  **SPEAKING** Look at the pictures and discuss the questions.

  1 What do the pictures illustrate?
  2 How was life in the past harder than it is today?

2 **Read the article quickly. Make notes on these questions about the Great Fire of London.**

1	In what year did it happen?
2	How did it start?
3	How long did it last?
4	How did people get away?
5	How was the fire stopped?
6	What damage did it do?

3 🔊 **1.13** **Read the article again and listen. Add details to your notes from Exercise 2.**

▮ TRAIN TO THiNK ▮

Following an idea through a paragraph

It can be difficult to follow what a writer is trying to say in a longer paragraph. We need to read carefully to understand fully what the writer is saying.

4 **Answer the questions.**

The end of Paragraph 2 says: "The situation provided the perfect conditions for flames to spread."

  1 Look back at the paragraph. How many things are needed to start a big fire? List them.
  2 What were those things in London in 1666?

The beginning of Paragraph 3 says: "The fire spread quickly, but it was also extremely difficult to fight."

  3 Look at the paragraph. Why was the fire difficult to fight?

The great fire of London
The event that changed the face of 17th-century London forever

It was 1 a.m. on Sunday, September 2, 1666. London was sleeping. In a small bakery in Pudding Lane, Thomas Farriner and his workers were busily making bread for the coming day when, suddenly, a fire broke out. Just four days later, thousands of houses had been destroyed and countless people were homeless. How did this happen, and why was the damage so extensive?

For a fire to start, three things are needed: a spark, fuel, and oxygen. In the bakery in Pudding Lane, a maid didn't tend to the ovens properly. They got too hot, and sparks began to fly. The weather that year had been extremely hot. It hadn't rained for months. But people knew winter was coming, so they'd stocked their cupboards with food and oil. Warehouses were full of wood, coal, and other winter supplies. A strong wind was blowing from the east. The situation provided the perfect conditions for flames to spread. What followed was one of the biggest disasters of the 17th-century world.

The fire spread quickly, but it was also extremely difficult to fight. It started in a poor area of the city, where houses were built very close to one another. Tens of thousands of people were living in very small spaces. A simple house was often home to many families as well as lodgers. As the catastrophe struck, people panicked. Some had to smash their doors to get out of their homes. The streets were blocked with people and with material that had fallen from houses. Many people had grabbed their most important possessions and were trying to flee from the flames with them. They screamed in terror and suffered from the heat and the smoke. Some escaped from the city on boats. Others simply dived into the river to save themselves.

The fire had raged for almost four days when the Duke of York put a plan into action. His soldiers demolished a large warehouse full of paper. This robbed the fire of more fuel and created a "fire break" that the flames could not jump over. At about this time, the wind also changed direction, driving the fire back into itself. At last, the flames died down enough to be controlled. The fire was finished.

Although surprisingly few people lost their lives, at least 13,000 houses – 80 percent of the city's buildings – had been destroyed. Thousands of people had become homeless and had lost everything they owned. Gradually, houses were rebuilt in the ruins, but this took several years. Many Londoners moved away from their city and never returned.

SPEAKING

Work in pairs. Discuss these questions.

1 What other events would you suggest for the *Events that shook the world* series? Why?
2 If you had to leave your home in a hurry and could only save three things, what would you choose?

GRAMMAR
Narrative tenses (review)

1 **Match the sentences from the article on page 21 with the tenses. One tense is used twice. Then complete the rule.**

 1 London **was sleeping**. ☐

 2 Thomas Farriner and his workers **were** busily **making** bread [...] when, suddenly, a fire broke out. ☐

 3 It **hadn't rained** for months. ☐

 4 His soldiers **demolished** a large warehouse. ☐

 a past perfect

 b simple past

 c past continuous

> **RULE:**
>
> We use the ...
>
> 1 _____ to talk about finished actions in the past.
>
> 2 _____ to talk about longer actions in the past interrupted by shorter actions.
>
> 3 _____ to set the scene.
>
> 4 _____ to talk about actions before a certain time in the past.

2 **Complete the sentences with the simple past or past continuous form of the verbs.**

 0 While people *were running* toward the river, a warehouse *exploded*. (run / explode)

 1 When they _____ how serious it was, they _____ their possessions and _____ away. (see / take / run)

 2 A man _____ for his family when he _____ a baby in the street. (look / find)

 3 While they _____ how to stop the fire, it _____ clear that little could be done. (think about / become)

 4 While the bakery workers _____ bread, a small fire _____. (make / start)

3 **Complete the conversation with the correct form of the verbs. Use the tenses from Exercise 1.**

 burn | do | see | run | sit | walk | go | open

 IAN Yesterday, as I ¹_____ up to our house, I ²_____ smoke coming from the window.

 ELI ³_____ something _____?

 IAN Luckily, no. I ⁴_____ up to the house, ⁵_____ the door, and there was my brother. He ⁶_____ on the floor in shock. He ⁷_____ science experiments! One of them ⁸_____ wrong and exploded.

Workbook page 18

VOCABULARY
Descriptive verbs

1 **Certain verbs make narratives sound more dramatic. Find these words in a dictionary. On a piece of paper, write down:**

 1 what they mean

 2 their simple past and past participle forms

 smash | rage | dive | flee | strike
 demolish | grab | scream

2 **Replace the underlined words with words from Exercise 1. Change the form if necessary.**

 0 He picked up a rock and <u>broke</u> the windshield of the car. *smashed*

 1 The thief stole a motorcycle and <u>escaped</u>. _____

 2 The fires had <u>burned</u> for days, and no one knew how to stop them. _____

 3 When I got there, I heard somebody <u>shouting</u> for help. _____

 4 They <u>tore down</u> the houses to make space for new stores. _____

 5 The man <u>quickly took</u> my wallet from me and ran away. _____

 6 The car lost control and <u>hit</u> another vehicle. _____

 7 He took off his coat and <u>jumped</u> into the water. _____

Workbook page 20

> ## Pronunciation
> Initial consonant clusters with /s/
> **Go to page 120.**

LISTENING

1 Look at the picture. Why do you think the cow was in court? Choose the best option.

A It was accused of hurting a human.

B It was interrupting a court meeting.

C A man was accused of hurting the cow.

2 🔊 1.16 Listen to Ryan's talk. Then answer the questions.

1 When were animals taken to court?

2 In which parts of the world did this happen?

3 🔊 1.16 Listen again. For questions 1–5, choose A, B, or C.

1 What were the French rats accused of?

A entering restaurants

B taking people's food

C hunting cats

2 According to the man, why didn't the rats accept their order to appear in court?

A They hadn't received it.

B They couldn't read it.

C They'd never accept an invitation from humans.

3 Why did he say the rats would never go to court?

A No one would understand them.

B They might not be safe.

C They couldn't be friends with humans.

4 How did the other people react to the man?

A They thought he was crazy.

B They laughed at him.

C They couldn't argue against him.

5 What happened to the rats?

A They were hunted and killed.

B They were found "not guilty."

C They were ordered to leave the village.

▌THiNK VALUES ▌

Animal rights

1 Read the scenarios. Match them with statements 1–6. There are two statements for each scenario.

Scenario A: ☐ / ☐

Work on a huge multi-million-dollar shopping mall has been stopped because nests of an extremely rare frog have been found in the area. It is one of only five places where this frog breeds. The real estate developers are putting pressure on the local government, saying it will be a disaster for the economy if they aren't allowed to finish the job.

Scenario B: ☐ / ☐

An elderly lady lives on her own. She has family, but they all live far away. A relative has suggested buying her a parrot for her 80th birthday. Other family members are against the idea of keeping an animal in a cage.

Scenario C: ☐ / ☐

There is a hotel that's very popular with tourists because it's close to a beautiful forest. The forest is home to a species of large spider. Although it's harmless, people working in the hotel have been given strict orders to kill any spiders that get into the guest rooms.

1 A bird in a cage can be a great companion for a person who lives alone, so it's the right present.

2 Creating places where people can vacation is more important than worrying about a few animals.

3 We can't afford to lose any species of animal.

4 Places where endangered animals have their natural habitat belong to the animals, and not to people.

5 Spiders are ugly and disgusting, and many people are scared of them. Of course they should be killed.

6 Birds need to fly, and they need space to be able to do that. Cages should be forbidden.

2 **SPEAKING** Which of the statements (1–6) do you agree with? Which do you disagree with? Why? Make notes about your answers. Then compare your ideas in pairs or small groups.

READING

1 Work in pairs. Look at the pictures, the title, and the paragraph headings. What information do you think each paragraph might contain?

2 Read the article and check your answers.

Family life
in 17th-century Britain

By the 17th century, life in Europe had started to be more comfortable for those who had money. Trade had become more important, and the number of people who could read and write was starting to grow. But while the rich were enjoying good food, poetry, and the theater, life for the poor hadn't changed much at all. Here are a few examples of what ordinary family life was like in the olden days.

A typical household

Women used to have seven or eight children, but typically one in every three children died before their first birthday. Many children had to leave home when they were as young as seven years old to work as shepherds or helpers on farms. There weren't many elderly people in the families because people died much younger than they usually do today. Few people expected to live beyond 40. In fact, children frequently grew up without parents at all.

A crowded life

Ordinary people used to live in one-room houses, along with their chickens, goats, even cows. Only richer families had mattresses. On cold nights, everyone in the family used to crowd together to sleep, to warm each other up. Unfortunately, this had a bad effect on people's health. Lice infestations were very common, and if one person suffered from an illness, everybody else got it, too.

Taking a bath was such a rare event that everybody smelled bad.

Childcare

Life didn't make it easy for people to spend a lot of time with their children. Parents used to leave even very young children on their own for most of the day. Records from that time report many stories of children who got too close to the fire and burned to death. But even when parents were with their children, they didn't care for them in the ways we're familiar with today. Children were often simply considered workers. Parents didn't use to sing songs to their children or play with them. It used to be normal to call a child "it" rather than "he" or "she."

It's easy to romanticize about the past and think how wonderfully simple life was compared to all the pressure we face in our day-to-day lives. But was it really so great? For most people, it probably wasn't.

3 Read the article again. Mark the sentences T (true) or F (false). Correct the false sentences.

1 Life in the 17th century was difficult for everybody, no matter how much money they had. ☐

2 Grandparents often used to live with families and look after the young children. ☐

3 There wasn't a lot of space in most people's homes, and they often shared it with their animals. ☐

4 Children sometimes died because their parents weren't or couldn't be concerned about their safety. ☐

5 Parents these days spend more time with their children than they did in the olden days. ☐

4 **SPEAKING** Work in pairs. Discuss these questions.

1 Compare family life in the 17th century with family life now. What are the most striking differences?

2 What do you think life will be like 100 years from now? Will it be easier? If so, how?

GRAMMAR
used to

1   **Complete these sentences from the article on page 24 with *used to* or *didn't use to*. Then complete the rule.**

   1   Women _____ have seven or eight children.
   2   On cold nights, everyone in the family _____ crowd together to sleep.
   3   Parents _____ sing songs to their children or play with them.
   4   It _____ be normal to call a child "it".

   > **RULE:** To talk about habits and repeated actions in the *past / present*, we can use *used to* or *didn't use to*.

2   **Complete the sentences and conversations with the correct form of *used to*.**

   0   My family ___*used to*___ go skiing every winter.
   1   We _____ have a car. We used to walk everywhere.
   2   A   _____ you _____ have a pet when you were a child?
       B   Yes, I _____ have a cat.
   3   A   _____ you _____ watch a lot of TV when you were younger?
       B   Yes, I _____ watch it every day when I got home from school.
   4   I _____ hate vegetables, but I love them now.
   5   A   _____ your dad _____ read you stories before you went to bed?
       B   No, he didn't, but my mom _____ .
   6   I _____ like having birthday parties. I was a really shy child.

   > Workbook page 19

VOCABULARY
Time periods

Look at phrases 1–9 and match them with categories a–c. Compare your answers with the class.

a   the present
b   the recent past
c   a long, long time ago in history

1	from 1995 until 2004
2	in the Middle Ages
3	in this day and age
4	these days
5	in the olden days
6	in the last century
7	not so long ago
8	a decade ago
9	nowadays

   > Workbook page 20

FUNCTIONS
Talking about the past

Work in pairs. Choose a topic for your partner and a period in the past. Your partner makes a comparison between the present and that time period. Take turns.

school | food | technology
games | home | travel

> games in the 1930s

> Well, children used to play with teddy bears or dolls. These days, many kids prefer video games.

Culture

1 **Look at the photos and answer the questions.**

  1 In what part of the world were these photos taken?

  2 Why might life be difficult there? How many reasons can you think of?

2 🔊 1.17 **Read and listen to the article. Check your predictions.**

Where life is really hard

It's the end of the winter. Most people have been inside for weeks. They haven't seen the sun for a long time. But some men are outside. It's bitterly cold, with temperatures of around -45° Celsius, and the freezing wind makes the situation difficult for them to bear. These men are hunters, and the survival of the people they've left behind in the villages depends on how successful their hunt is.

Akycha is one of these men. He's been out hunting for more than a week now. While he's away from home, he stays overnight in a little igloo that he's made himself from ice and snow. The igloo protects him from the freezing wind. Inside, there's a little stove for cooking, and a small stone lamp, which provides light. Together, they help to create a temperature of around 12° Celsius.

Right now, Akycha is several kilometers away from his igloo. He's riding his snowmobile along the coast, far out on the frozen sea. Suddenly, he can see something in the distance. He stops his snowmobile and checks through his binoculars. It's a seal. Holding a screen of white canvas in front of him with one hand and his gun in the other, he moves forward, cautiously hiding behind the screen all the time so that the seal won't notice him. If he's lucky and his hunt goes well, the meat he brings home should last his family for several weeks.

Akycha and his people are part of the Inuit community. Most of them still live a very traditional life, a life that makes them dependent on hunting seals and whales. Some of them also live off the reindeer they keep.

The Inuit are indigenous people of the Arctic Circle, which means their ancestors were the first people to live on this land. The Arctic Circle is a huge land area that belongs to a number of northern countries: Russia, the U.S., Canada, Greenland, Norway, Sweden, Finland, and Iceland. The northern environment is an exceptional habitat. Temperatures are low during most of the year, and summers are short, which means that plants can only grow for a few weeks every year. If the reindeer eat the moss that grows in a certain area, it can take up to 30 years for the plants to grow back. This is why Inuits who make a living from keeping and breeding reindeer have to be constantly on the move with their herds.

For most of us, life is less hard than it is for the Inuit people. But maybe we can learn something from them. Their traditional way of life is a model of living in partnership with nature rather than exploiting and destroying it.

3 **Read the article again. Answer the questions.**

  1 What are winters like inside the Arctic Circle?

  2 How does Akycha survive when he's out hunting?

  3 What does he hunt, and how does he do this?

  4 Why can't the Inuit who keep reindeer stay in one place for a long time?

4 **SPEAKING** **Work in pairs. Discuss these questions.**

  1 In what other areas of the world do people live under extreme conditions?

  2 What is the coldest or hottest place you've ever been in? What was the experience like for you?

  3 Would you find it easier to live in an area where it's very cold or very hot?

5 VOCABULARY There are eight highlighted words or phrases in the article. Match them with these definitions.

1 continue to be enough _____
2 not taken with them _____
3 from one evening through to the next morning _____
4 not staying in one place for very long _____
5 tolerate, put up with _____
6 large groups of animals _____
7 a type of plant _____
8 raising (animals) _____

WRITING

A magazine article about a historic event

1 Read the article. What happened in Berlin in these years?

1 1961   2 1989   3 1990

2 Find examples in the article of:

1 a sentence containing the simple past and the past continuous.
2 the past perfect.
3 descriptive verbs.
4 expressions referring back to the past.

3 The article has three paragraphs. Which of them:

a sets the scene for the main events? ☐
b describes the main action? ☐
c describes the historical background? ☐

4 Think of an event that shook the world.

- Do some Internet research to find out more about it.
- Choose the most important and interesting details.
- Organize the information into paragraphs.
- Think about the language you'll need to describe the event.

5 Write an article for a school magazine about an event that shook the world (about 200 words).

The fall of the Berlin Wall

For 28 years, Berlin was a divided city. Ever since its construction in 1961, a huge wall had stopped citizens from East Germany from going to the West. Many people had tried. Some were successful, but many more died, shot as they attempted to get to the other side.

In 1989, there were a number of radical political demonstrations across Central and Eastern Europe. The people of countries such as Poland and Hungary protested against their governments and managed to change them. On November 9, the East German government announced that their people were free to go to the western side of the city.

That evening, thousands of East Berliners rushed to the wall and demanded that the border guards open the gates. The guards didn't know what to do. While the crowds were singing, the guards called their bosses for orders. It soon became clear that they had no choice but to let the people pass. On the other side, they were greeted by West Berliners with flowers and champagne. People climbed on top of the wall and began dancing on it to celebrate their new freedom. People started arriving with sledgehammers to try to smash the wall. Many grabbed bricks as souvenirs. A little later, the government sent in bulldozers to demolish the wall. The wall that had divided a city for nearly three decades was soon gone, and, 339 days later, the two nations of East and West Germany also became one.

READING AND USE OF ENGLISH
Part 1: Multiple-choice cloze

Workbook page 17

1   For questions 1–8, read the text below and decide which answer (A, B, C, or D) best fills each blank. There is an example at the beginning (0).

0   A (stopped)   B   finished   C   ended   D   not

Do you ever stop and think about how easy the Internet has made our lives? I know there are times when it's slow or has (0) ___ working altogether, times when maybe you feel like (1) ___ your computer screen into tiny pieces. But just think of all those things you use it for. You want to buy the new song – you can (2) ___ online and download it. You need to (3) ___ some research for your homework – you can find it all there on the Web. You feel (4) ___ chatting with your best friend, so you Skype them. You just want a (5) ___ from your homework, so you start up Minecraft or whatever game is your favorite and start playing. These (6) ___ everything we need is just a click away.

Of course, it wasn't always like this. Only a few decades (7) ___, people had to do things like go to the store if they wanted to buy something – and sometimes the store was closed! They had to look in very large, heavy books called encyclopedias to find information. They had to (8) ___ up the telephone if they wanted to talk – and if their best friend wasn't home, they simply couldn't talk to them. That's how tough life was. And these poor people who had to suffer such hardships were … our parents! Makes you feel sorry for them, doesn't it?

1	A	demolishing	B	striking	C	smashing	D grabbing
2	A	come	B	enter	C	click	D go
3	A	do	B	make	C	find	D ask
4	A	about	B	like	C	of	D to
5	A	break	B	stop	C	end	D fix
6	A	times	B	ages	C	years	D days
7	A	after	B	since	C	ago	D past
8	A	take	B	pick	C	grab	D hold

SPEAKING
Part 1: Interview

Workbook page 25

2   In pairs, ask and answer the questions.

1   Who do you spend the most time with on weekends, and what do you do with them?
2   What kind of movies do you like most? What do you like about them?
3   Where did you go on your last vacation? What was it like?
4   What's your favorite sport to play? What do you like about it?
5   What things do you enjoy doing the most with your parents?
6   What is your favorite room in your home, and why do you like it?
7   If you could be anywhere right now, where would you be, and why?
8   What things do you like to do at home on a rainy day?
9   Who is your best friend, and what do you like the most about him/her?

VOCABULARY

1 Complete the sentences with the words in the list. There are four extra words.

break | change | do | form | grab | make | quit
scream | retire | settle | smash | strike | struggle | travel

1   It would be wonderful to _____ around the world one day.

2   It's a really bad habit. I need to _____ it soon.

3   He always used to arrive late, and no one could make him _____ his ways.

4   Good luck with the test. I'm sure you'll _____ really well.

5   Every December 31, I _____ a resolution to do something, but I usually break it!

6   I saw a man _____ that woman's purse and run away.

7   On her 65th birthday, she decided to _____ and travel the world.

8   I need more time to study for my exams, so I'm going to _____ my judo classes for a while.

9   I think he's going to break that window. Oh, no! He's going to _____ it!

10 They were so excited by the concert that they started to _____ really loudly. ___ /10

GRAMMAR

2 Complete the sentences with the phrases in the list. There are two extra phrases.

was looking | used to look | 'm seeing | are going to | go to | used to love | see | 'll love

1   I _____ my aunt and uncle once a month.

2   Four or five of us _____ eat pizza tonight.

3   Have fun at the concert – I'm sure you _____ it!

4   When I was a kid, I _____ going to the river to swim.

5   I'm not very well, so I _____ the doctor tomorrow.

6   When I saw her, she _____ in a store window.

3 Find and correct the mistake in each sentence.

1   When he was young, my dad used to reading stories. _____

2   I got there at 4, but no one was there. The party finished! _____

3   I am running in the park every morning before school. _____

4   We're so excited because we will go on vacation next week. _____

5   After the train doors closed, it had started to move. _____

6   While I was riding in the park, I was falling off my bike. _____ ___ /12

FUNCTIONAL LANGUAGE

4 Circle the correct words.

1   **A** I'm angry with Jack. He's *always / often* picking on me.

    B I know. He's horrible. *I don't like / I'm not liking* him at all.

2   **A** You know, in the *past / olden* days, people didn't have the Internet.

    B I know! But *these days / not so long ago* we can get information so quickly!

3   **A** Gina and I *have / are having* lunch tomorrow. Why don't you come, too?

    B Great – thank you! *I see / I'll see* you at the restaurant! ___ /8

4   **A** No one *uses / is using* typewriters anymore.

    B Not in *nowadays / this day and age*, no!

MY SCORE	___ /30
22 – 30	
10 – 21	
0 – 9	

OBJECTIVES

FUNCTIONS: giving advice; expressing obligation; giving recommendations, warnings, and prohibitions

GRAMMAR: *(don't) have to / ought to / should(n't) / must; had better (not); can('t) / must (not)*

VOCABULARY: making and selling; expressions with *name*

READING

1 Look at the names and logos and answer the questions.

   1 These are the names and logos of various companies. What kind of products do they offer?

> *Jaguar sells cars.*

   2 What are two more names of companies or products that are famous around the world?

2 **SPEAKING** Work in pairs. Some people think the name of a brand is very important. What do you think is the reason for this?

3 Read the blog entry quickly. Which of the brands shown above does it mention?

4 **◄⑴ 1.18** Read the blog entry again and listen. Answer the questions.

   1 Why do companies think a lot about a brand name?

   2 What makes a good brand name?

   3 Why were each of these names chosen?

     Jaguar | Pret A Manger | WhatsApp

   4 Why do some teenagers choose to buy more expensive products (like clothes)?

▌TRAIN TO THiNK ▌

Identifying the main topic of a paragraph

Writers use a new paragraph when they want to change the topic. The opening line of a paragraph usually gives you a clue about its topic.

5 Look at paragraphs 3 and 4. What is the topic of each paragraph?

   A what teenagers wear to school ☐

   B brand names are important in the teenage market ☐

   C some really bad brand names ☐

   D ways to pick a brand name ☐

Brand names

1 Imagine you've thought of a great idea for a product to make and sell – a game or an app or some clothes, for example. You just know that you can sell millions of them, but first of all, you must give the product a name – a brand name. And that may not be as easy as you think.

2 The brand name is the thing that distinguishes your product from all others, and it's really important that it makes an impact. Businesses spend a lot of time thinking about brand names. After the name has been picked, it's very difficult to change, so companies have to get it right from the start.

3 So how do you choose a name? A brand name ought to be unique, memorable, and easy to understand. It should create some kind of emotional connection with people who buy the product – the target market. Some companies use a family name. When Henry Ford started making cars, he just called the company Ford. But you don't have to use a family name. You can go for an image. Staying with cars, think about the brand name Jaguar, a beautiful but dangerous wild cat. What does that say about the manufacturer's product? And then some companies use wordplay. It's a common technique for naming apps, for example, WhatsApp (from the English expression *What's up?*). Others like to use foreign words because they sound special or different. For example, in Britain and the U.S., there's a chain of sandwich shops with the French name Pret A Manger, which means "ready to eat." You should also think about where your product will be sold. You shouldn't choose a name that might not work in certain countries or cultures.

There's a famous story about a car company that launched a new car called the Nova. They thought it suggested something powerful and new, but in Spanish it could be read as *no va* or "it doesn't go." (This story isn't actually true, but it is such a good example of a possible problem that business school professors still tell it to their students!)

4 These days, the choice of brand name is particularly important if your product is targeted at the teen market. Teenage consumers are typically more concerned with brand names and company logos than any other group. When a brand, especially a clothing brand, becomes popular with teenagers, there's a lot of pressure to wear those clothes and have the name and/or logo visible. A teacher in an American high school said, "I certainly see that kids are obsessed with brand names. They won't buy something that's almost identical – and cheaper – simply because they feel they must wear something with the right logo." So if you want to get into the teenage market, you have to find a product and a brand name that works with that age group and create some great ads, too.

5 Companies know that the name isn't everything – the product itself has to be good, of course – but it's an essential part of the package.

"I'm so glad that we don't have to wear school uniforms anymore!"

SPEAKING

Work in pairs. Discuss these questions.

1 Can you think of other brand names that:
   a use a family name?
   b try to create an image?
   c are in another language?
2 Have you ever bought or wanted something just because of the brand? Give examples.

GRAMMAR

(don't) have to / ought to / should(n't) / must

1   **Complete the sentences from the article on page 31. Then complete the rule with the correct modals.**

1   First of all, you _____ give the product a name.

2   Companies _____ get it right from the start.

3   A brand name _____ be unique, memorable, and easy to understand.

4   But you _____ use a family name.

5   You _____ also think about where your product will be sold.

6   You _____ choose a name that might not work in certain countries or cultures.

> **RULE:** We use
> 1 _____ or *must* to say "this is important or necessary."
> 2 _____ to say "this isn't important or necessary."
> *should* or 3 _____ to tell someone that something is a good idea.
> 4 _____ to tell someone that something isn't a good idea.
> Note: (*Ought to* isn't as common as *should*. It's used mostly in writing, and the negative form is rare.)

2   **Complete the dialogue with the correct form of (don't) have to.**

MARIA   Mom, there's a new phone out. It's awesome. I ¹_____ get one!

MOM   Your phone is fine. You ²_____ buy another one.

MARIA   But you know what it's like at school. Everyone ³_____ have the latest version!

MOM   Yes, and it's terrible. Why ⁴_____ you all _____ wear the same clothes, for example?

MARIA   Because it's what teenagers do.

MOM   But I ⁵_____ go to work to pay for all these things, right?

MARIA   Oh, Mom! You ⁶_____ be so difficult!

3   **Complete the conversation with suitable modal verbs. There is often more than one possible answer.**

JILL   The new café is great. You¹_____ go there. You ²_____ try the muffins. They're delicious!

JACK   OK. What's the place called, anyway?

JILL   Can you believe it's called The Coffee Shop?!

JACK   What a boring name! You ³_____ be a genius to think of that!

JILL   They ⁴_____ have a foreign name.

JACK   Well, OK. But it ⁵_____ be easy to pronounce. There's a store in town called Arighi Bianchi, and no one knows how to say it.

JILL   But the owner is Italian. It's his name!

JACK   I guess I ⁶_____ know that. Anyway, I ⁷_____ go home and do my homework for tomorrow.

JILL   You ⁸_____ worry about that. It's easy.

JACK   Really? OK, so let's go to the movies. There's a new comedy that we ⁹_____ see!

Workbook page 28

VOCABULARY
Making and selling

1   **Complete the sentences with the words.**

advertisements (ads) | brand | chain consumers | image | logo | manufacturer products

1   They make cleaning _____, like laundry detergent.

2   The prices have gone up a lot, so now _____ have to pay more.

3   I always buy the same _____ of shoes because they're so comfortable.

4   It's a _____ of stores in the U.S.

5   I love their _____ on TV.

6   The Nike _____ is a large check mark.

7   When the company's director went to prison, it damaged the company's _____.

8   If it doesn't work, send it back to the _____.

2   **SPEAKING Answer the questions. Then work in pairs and compare your answers.**

Can you name …

1   three places where you usually see ads?

2   a manufacturer of cell phones?

3   a chain of stores and a chain of restaurants?

4   one thing you always buy the same brand of?

Workbook page 30

LISTENING

1 **◀》1.19** **Listen to Paul talking to his teacher, Mrs. Jenkins. What is their conversation about?** (Circle) **the correct option.**

   A how to remember names
   B why some names are hard to remember
   C why some people can't remember names

2 **◀》1.19** **Listen again. Mark the sentences T (true) or F (false).**

   1 Mrs. Jenkins has taught Paul's class three times. ☐
   2 Paul isn't good at remembering people's names. ☐
   3 Mrs. Jenkins says you have to concentrate if you want to remember names. ☐

   4 Mrs. Jenkins thinks it's useful to say the person's name as soon as you hear it. ☐
   5 She remembered Paul's name because she knows another person named Paul. ☐
   6 She always remembers people's names. ☐

GRAMMAR
had better (not)

1 **Complete these sentences from the listening. Then** (circle) **the correct words to complete the rule.**

   1 I _____ go now.
   2 You _____ be late for class.

   > **RULE:** We use *had ('d) better* to warn someone that bad things will happen if they [1]*do / don't do* something. We use *had ('d) better not* to warn someone that bad things will happen if they [2]*do / don't do* something.

2 **Complete the sentences with *had better (not)*.**

   1 The bus leaves in two minutes. You _____ run.
   2 I'll lend you my pen, but you _____ break it!
   3 It's going to rain. We _____ go inside.
   4 You have to get up very early tomorrow, so you _____ go to bed. It's 1 a.m.
   5 You _____ eat any more candy. You'll be sick.

   → Workbook page 29

FUNCTIONS
Giving advice

1 **◀》1.20** **Put the sentences in the correct order to make two dialogues. Then listen and check.**

   1 ☐ LIAM Why? What's her name?
      ☐ LIAM What's the matter, Jen?
      ☐ LIAM Well, you'd better get some help – quickly!
      ☐ JEN It's something like Sharita Wass Ikonor.
      ☐ JEN I have to call someone, and I have no idea how to pronounce her name.

   2 ☐ BOB Well, I misspelled her son's name in his birthday card. His name's Allen. It's A-L-L-E-N, and I wrote A-L-A-N.
      ☐ BOB I know. She's really mad.
      ☐ BOB My sister's really angry with me.
      ☐ MIA Why?
      ☐ MIA You'd better not do that again!

2 **Work in pairs. Imagine you forgot your best friend's birthday. Write a conversation using *had better (not)*.**

▌THiNK SELF-ESTEEM ▌
People and their names

1 **Complete the questionnaire (1 = I strongly agree; 5 = I strongly disagree).**

   1 I find it easy to remember people's names. ☐
   2 I only remember the names of people I like. ☐
   3 I hate it when people forget my name. ☐
   4 Your name is an important part of who you are. ☐
   5 I feel sorry for people who have unusual names. ☐

2 **SPEAKING** Compare your answers in small groups. Which question(s) do you agree on?

READING

1 Look at the names and answer the questions.

Apple Martin | Brooklyn Beckham | Moon Unit Zappa

1 Do you know anything about these people?

2 Think of one thing that they have in common.

2 These are eight names that parents tried to give their children. Check (✓) the names that you think were allowed.

☐ 1 Talula Does the Hula From Hawaii

☐ 2 Fish and Chips

☐ 3 Number 16 Bus Shelter

☐ 4 Google

☐ 5 Ikea

☐ 6 Q

☐ 7 Pluto

☐ 8 Monkey

Brooklyn Beckham

Moon Unit Zappa

3 Read the article and check your answers to Exercise 2.

4 Read the article again. Answer the questions.

1 Which people's unusual names do we often hear about?

2 What reason did a New Zealand judge give for not allowing some names?

3 What did Mariléia dos Santos decide to do?

4 What did she become well known for?

5 Why did David Carradine give his son an unusual name?

5 SPEAKING Mark each statement with a number from 1 to 5 (1 = I strongly agree; 5 = I strongly disagree).

a Parents should be able to give their children any name they want. ☐

b Children with silly names should be allowed to change them when they're 12 years old. ☐

c It doesn't matter what name a child has because she or he can change it as an adult. ☐

d Every country should have a list of names that parents are allowed to give their children. ☐

6 SPEAKING Compare your answers with a partner.

Crazy names

Names for your children: It's always a big question for parents. Should you give them an "ordinary" name, or do you want something a little different? We always hear about big names in the world of entertainment and sports who choose something that isn't ordinary. They give their kids names like Apple or Brooklyn or Moon Unit. Other people like to use brand names for their children, so there are now quite a few people named Armani or Diesel running around on school playgrounds.

Can you name your child anything you want? That depends on where you live. In New Zealand, for example, you can't name your child Talula Does the Hula From Hawaii, and you can't name your twins Fish and Chips. (And yes, parents in New Zealand really have tried to give their kids these names.) It's hard to believe, but you *can* name a child Number 16 Bus Shelter. Generally, certain names aren't allowed because, as a New Zealand judge said in one case, "a name must not make a fool of the child."

In Sweden, if you want the name Google for your kid, then go ahead, no problem. But you'd better not try to name your children Ikea or Q because the government won't let you.

Things are even more difficult in Denmark. There's an official list of about 7,000 approved names, and parents need to get special permission to use a name that isn't on it. Pluto and Monkey aren't on it.

Of course, when kids grow up, they can decide to change their name and then it's a different game altogether. If a female soccer player wants to call herself Michael Jackson, which is what Brazilian player Mariléia dos Santos decided to do, then there's nothing to stop her. (She made a name for herself as one of the best players in the world.) And of course, pop stars do it all the time. Shawn Corey Carter and Stefani Germanotta, for example, might not be household names today if they hadn't decided to use the stage names Jay-Z and Lady Gaga. Some people, however, change their name from something unusual to something ordinary in order to blend in. David Carradine named his son Free because he wanted him to feel free to do anything, even to change his name – which he did, to Tom.

GRAMMAR
can('t) / must (not)

1 Complete these sentences from the listening on page 33 and the article on page 34. Then complete the rule with *can*, *can't*, and *must (not)*.

1 _____ I ask you something?
2 You _____ name your twins Fish and Chips.
3 You _____ name a child Number 16 Bus Shelter.
4 A name "_____ make a fool of the child."

> **RULE:** To talk or ask about permission, we often use the modal verb [1]_____. To say what isn't allowed, we often use [2]_____ or _____ .

2 Complete the sentences with *must not* and the verbs. Then match them with the pictures.

run | talk | be | miss

1 You _____ so loudly!
2 I _____ late.
3 I _____ the goal!
4 You _____ .

3 Rewrite the sentences in your notebook using modal verbs from this unit and the pronouns in parentheses. There is often more than one possible answer.

0 Diving isn't allowed. (you)
You can't dive here.
1 It isn't necessary for us to wear uniforms. (we)
2 It's a good idea to buy a new phone. (you)
3 It's OK for you to use my laptop. (you)
4 It's necessary for them to work harder. (they)
5 Is it OK to play here? (we)

Workbook page 29

VOCABULARY
Expressions with *name*

1 Match the underlined expressions with the definitions.

1 Tony Hawk is <u>a big name</u> in skateboarding. ☐
2 He's upset because some of the other kids <u>call him names</u>. ☐
3 Jay-Z isn't his real name – it's his <u>stage name</u>. ☐
4 Fish, meat, vegetables, fruit – <u>you name it</u>, I eat it. ☐
5 Look! It's <u>what's-his-name</u>. ☐
6 I know you don't want to take the tests, but it's <u>the name of the game</u> for getting into college. ☐
7 He <u>made a name for himself</u> in the world of advertising. ☐

a a man whose name I can't remember
b the most important part of something
c a person who is important or famous in their profession
d a name that a person (usually an actor or a singer) uses in their profession
e use rude names about, or to, a person
f become known or respected by many people
g anything you say (or choose)

2 Complete the missing word(s).

1 She's been to Europe, Asia, and Australia – you _____ _____ , she's been there!
2 Hard work is the _____ of _____ _____ if you want to do well on your tests.
3 My uncle's a doctor. He's a _____ _____ in the field of cancer research.
4 Some of her classmates _____ her _____. It's horrible for her.
5 Oh look! There's _____-his-_____. You know, that boy who lives on your street.
6 She made _____ _____ for _____ on a reality TV show and became a famous singer.
7 Bruno Mars is the _____ name of Pete Gene Hernandez.

Workbook page 30

> ### Pronunciation
> Strong and weak forms: /ɑv/ and /əv/
> **Go to page 120.**

Fiction

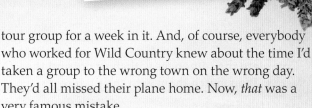

1 ◀)) 1.23 **Read and listen to the introduction and the first part of the extract. Answer the questions.**

1 What is Tess's full name?
2 In the company her name is used to mean something. What, and why?

Wild Country by Margaret Johnson

Tess and Grant are tour guides for a group walking tour in France. But they don't get along very well – at least not at first …

"I didn't ask to work with you," Grant said, "and I know you didn't ask to work with me. But here we are, so why don't we at least try to get along with each other?" I looked back at him angrily. "I'll try if you try," I said, but I didn't like the smile he gave me.

I'd been a tour guide for Wild Country, my father's walking tour company, for a year. In that time I'd been late meeting a group at the airport several times. I'd also lost my wallet, with all the money to buy food for the tour group for a week in it. And, of course, everybody who worked for Wild Country knew about the time I'd taken a group to the wrong town on the wrong day. They'd all missed their plane home. Now, *that* was a very famous mistake.

My mistakes were so famous in the company that doing something wrong was called "doing a Tess Marriot." I think it was Grant Cooper who started saying that, actually – awful man.

2 ◀)) 1.24 **Read and listen to the second part of the extract. Mark the sentences T (true) or F (false).**

1 Tess thinks her father's idea was a bad one. ☐
2 She's happy when she arrives at the airport. ☐
3 She tries hard to smile when she enters the airport. ☐
4 She likes Grant because he laughs a lot. ☐
5 She helps Grant find the group of tourists. ☐

And now my father had arranged for me to work with Grant Cooper on this tour. He thought I would learn something from Grant – something to make me a better tour guide. I thought my father was wrong. I was just too different from Grant, and I didn't want to be like him, anyway.

After 30 minutes in a hot bus with these thoughts going around and around in my head, I felt very fed up, which was the opposite of how I should feel when meeting a group at the start of a tour.

A tour guide should smile as often as possible. That's what it said in the book I was given when I started the job. *At the beginning of a tour, people are often tired from their trip. They may also be worried about what the other people on the tour will be like. A smile from you makes everybody feel better.*

So as I entered the airport, I tried to put a smile on my face. But it was difficult to keep it there as I tried, without luck, to find my group.

"Wild Country, Walking in Provence?" I asked any group of more than four people, but they all looked at me as if I was crazy. I was beginning to think I'd gotten the time wrong or come to the wrong airport when I saw him – Grant Cooper. My heart immediately jumped, and not just because I was nervous about being late. I didn't like Grant, but he was very good-looking. I'd liked the look of him when I first met him. But then I'd spoken to him, and all that changed. I just didn't find him easy to get along with. Every time he spoke to me I felt he was laughing at me. It made me so mad I wanted to scream.

As I got closer, I could see that Grant had already found the group. There was nothing else to do but walk up to them with a big Wild Country smile on my face.

"Hello, everybody," I said. "I'm Tess Marriot, one of your tour guides. I hope you had a good trip?"

"Hello, Tess," Grant said. "Did you get lost on your way to the airport?"

3 SPEAKING Work in pairs. Discuss these questions.

1 Imagine you're Tess. What's your answer to Grant's question at the end of the extract?

2 In the extract we learn that "doing a Tess Marriot" means making a mistake.

   a Think of a famous person who is well known for certain actions or qualities. How could that person's name be used?

> *I think "doing a Beyoncé" could mean singing really well and dancing at the same time.*

   b How would you like *your* name to be used?

WRITING
A reply to a letter asking for advice

1 Read the letter and the reply. Answer the questions.

   1 What is Alan's problem?
   2 What question does Susannah suggest that Alan ask himself?

2 Complete the missing words from Susannah's reply.

   1 This is the first question you _____ _____ ask yourself.
   2 If the answer is no, then maybe _____ _____ end the friendship now.
   3 ... you _____ _____ talk to him about the name-calling ...
   4 ... and explain that he _____ _____ stop saying those things.
   5 Finally, _____ _____ _____ _____ to talk to your parents.

3 Read Susannah's reply again. In which paragraph does she ...

   a offer advice to make the friendship work? ☐
   b outline Alan's problem? ☐
   c tell him to speak to others about his problem? ☐
   d ask Alan to think more carefully about the situation? ☐

4 Read another letter to Susannah. Write three pieces of advice for Lara.

5 Write a reply to Lara (150–200 words). Say what you think she should do.

Susannah's **advice page**

Write about a problem and Susannah will give you advice. This week's letter is from Alan in California.

Dear Susannah,

Last month we moved to a new town. My parents quickly made friends with the people who live next door. They have a son about my age. He's friendly and invites me to do things with him. But the thing is, when we see other kids, he calls them names and makes awful comments. He wants me to join in, but I don't want to.

What can I do? If I tell my parents, it'll be hard because they really like his parents. And to be honest, I don't have many other friends yet. If I stop hanging out with him, maybe he'll start calling me names, too.

What should I do?

Alan, California

Dear Alan,

It's often difficult to make new friends when you move, so it was almost perfect that your new neighbors had a son your age and that he wanted to be your friend. What a shame that you're finding it difficult to spend time with him.

You don't say in your letter if you think you could be friends if his behavior was better. This is the first question you ought to ask yourself. If the answer is no, then maybe you'd better end the friendship now. Don't worry – I'm sure you'll soon make lots of friends when you start school.

However, if you think you could be friends, then you should definitely talk to him about the name-calling and explain that he had better stop saying those things. If he's going to be a good friend, he'll listen to you. If he ignores you, then this friendship probably isn't going to work.

Finally, it's a good idea to talk to your parents. They're the people who know you best and are often the best people to give you advice.

Good luck!

Susannah

Dear Susannah,

I have very bad eyesight and need to wear thick glasses. Because of this, some people at school call me names. I tried not to let it bother me too much, but the problem is that it happens a lot. I've always enjoyed school and had lots of friends, but I'm starting to hate going there. My grades are also getting worse and some of the teachers have said they're disappointed in me. I know I should talk to the teachers, but I'm sure this is only going to make things worse. Can you help?

Lara, Miami

READING

1 Read the definition. Then look at the pictures. What dilemmas do you think they show?

> **dilemma:** a situation in which a difficult choice has to be made between two or more alternatives

2 Read the quiz quickly. Match each picture with a question.

3 🔊 1.25 Read the quiz again and listen. Then complete it with your answers. Compare with a partner.

4 **Match these responses with the quiz questions.**

☐ a I'd try to fix it before she noticed.

☐ b I'd keep quiet but make sure I worked really hard for my next test.

☐ c I'd ask if I could exchange it for another one.

☐ d I'd write my own answer but then look at her paper to check it.

☐ e I'd ask him or her what it was about.

☐ f I'd admit I didn't have enough money and ask to borrow some from a friend.

☐ g I'd have an argument with them about it.

☐ h I'd spend some of it and give some to charity.

What would YOU do?

What would you do if ...

1 you heard a text message arrive on your girlfriend's or boyfriend's phone when he or she was out of the room?

A I wouldn't open it.

B I'd read it and pretend I hadn't.

2 you found $100 in a cash machine outside a bank?

A I'd go into the bank and give it to someone who worked there.

B I'd keep it and buy myself something nice.

3 you noticed your teacher had made a mistake grading your test and given you a better grade?

A I'd tell my teacher about the mistake immediately.

B I wouldn't say anything.

4 you broke your mom's vase while playing soccer in the house?

A I'd own up to it and say it was me.

B I'd say that the cat did it.

5 you bought a shirt, wore it to a party once, and decided you didn't really like it?

A I'd give it to a friend.

B I'd take it back to the store, say I'd never worn it, and get my money back.

6 there was a party you really wanted to go to, but you thought your parents might not let you go?

A I'd be open, tell them why I wanted to go, and accept their decision.

B I'd say I was going to a friend's house, go to the party, and hide the truth from them.

7 you were taking a difficult math test and noticed that you could easily copy from your friend's paper?

A I wouldn't look. I'd just try harder to answer the questions myself.

B I'd look at her paper.

8 you didn't have enough money for a full-price movie ticket?

A I'd leave and go home.

B I'd lie about my age and try to get in for a cheaper price.

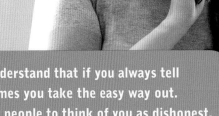

RESULTS

MORE As THAN Bs: You're basically an honest person. You understand that if you always tell the truth, people will trust you.   **MORE Bs THAN As:** Sometimes you take the easy way out. Be careful because it may cause you problems. You don't want people to think of you as dishonest.

▮TRAIN TO THiNK▮

Thinking of consequences

In order to make a good decision, it's important to think of all possible consequences for others and for yourself.

5 Choose four of the questions in the quiz. Think of possible consequences for each option.

Question	Action	Consequence
1	I read the text message.	My boyfriend gets angry and doesn't trust me anymore. We stop being friends.
	I don't read the text message.	I don't find out what the message is about.

SPEAKING

Work in pairs. Discuss these questions.

1 Which of the situations in the quiz is the most serious? Which is the least serious?

2 Do you agree with what the results say about you?

GRAMMAR
First and second conditional (review)

1 Complete these sentences from the quiz on page 39 with the correct forms of the verbs. Then match them with the parts of the rule.

1 What _____ you _____ (do) if you _____ (break) your mom's vase while playing soccer?

2 If you always _____ (tell) the truth, people _____ (trust) you.

> **RULE:** We use first conditional to talk about real situations and their consequences. We form it with an *if* + present simple / future (*will*) clause. _____
>
> We use second conditional to talk about hypothetical or very unlikely situations and their outcomes. We form it with *if* + past simple / *would* clause. _____

2 Complete the conditional sentences with the correct forms of the verbs. Think carefully about whether each one is a first or second conditional.

What should I do?

Why is Jan so mean to me? If Jan ¹_____ (not be) so mean to me, I ²_____ (want) to invite her to my party. The problem is, she's so popular. If she ³_____ (not have) so many friends, nobody ⁴_____ (care) if she was at my party or not. I have to invite her.

If I ⁵_____ (not invite) Jan to my party, nobody ⁶_____ (come) to it.

Maybe I shouldn't have a party. But if I ⁷_____ (not have) a party, I ⁸_____ (not get) any presents, and I want presents! Why are birthdays always so hard? If it ⁹_____ (not be) my birthday next week, my life ¹⁰_____ (not be) so complicated. If I ¹¹_____ (know) what to do, I ¹²_____ (do) it. But I don't!

Workbook page 36

Time conjunctions

3 Complete the sentences with the words.

if | until | when | as soon as

1 I don't know where he is, but I'll tell him _____ I see him.

2 I'm meeting him later, so I'll tell him _____ I see him.

3 It's really important. I'm going to tell him _____ I see him.

4 I'll work _____ he arrives and then I'll stop.

4 Complete the sentences so that they are true for you. Tell your partner.

1 As soon as I get home tonight, I …

2 If the weather is good this weekend, I …

3 When I'm 18, I …

4 I'm going to save all my money until …

Workbook page 36

VOCABULARY
Being honest

1 In your notebook, make a chart and categorize these terms as positive or negative.

~~cheat~~ | get away with something | lie
hide the truth | do the right thing
tell a lie | be open about something
tell the truth | own up to something

2 Complete the conversation with the words and phrases from Exercise 1.

DAN I have a problem. The other day I ⁰ *cheated* on a test. I copied from Ben.

ANA Why?

DAN I thought I could ¹_____ away with it, but now the teacher wants to know who copied who.

ANA You should ²_____ up to it and say it was you.

DAN I know, but it's too hard to ³_____ the truth.

ANA But you can't ⁴_____ to your teacher! And what about Ben? You can't ⁵_____ the truth from him either. He may be punished, too, you know.

DAN I could ⁶_____ her a lie and say it's just a coincidence that our papers are exactly the same.

ANA No. You need to be ⁷_____ about this.

DAN You're right, of course. It's just so hard to ⁸_____ the right thing sometimes.

Workbook page 38

LISTENING

1 **SPEAKING** Work in pairs. Look at the photos. What do you know about these people and characters? What difficulties might they face?

2 🔊 1.26 Listen to the conversation. What are the teenagers doing?

3 🔊 1.26 Listen again. Circle the
✳ correct answers.

1 Where are the teenagers?
   A on a long train trip
   B on the platform, waiting for a train
   C at home

2 What do they decide to play?
   A a card game invented by Madison
   B a guessing game invented by Liam
   C a traditional children's game

3 Why isn't Andy Murray a good choice for this game?
   A Madison and Susie don't like tennis.
   B He isn't famous enough.
   C He isn't a fictional character.

4 Why does Liam get angry when Madison guesses Superman?
   A He chose someone too easy.
   B She doesn't let him finish.
   C She got the wrong answer.

Superman

Andy Murray

Juliet (from *Romeo and Juliet*)

5 Why can't Liam guess Juliet?
   A He doesn't know who Juliet is.
   B He doesn't know very much about history.
   C He gets angry with Madison.

6 Why doesn't Madison say "Harry Potter" right away?
   A She's enjoying annoying Liam.
   B She doesn't know who it is.
   C She's bored with the game.

GRAMMAR
wish and *if only*

1 **Read the sentences. Which fictional characters might say them? Complete the rule. Use the sentences to help you.**

1 "I wish I **could** kill Lord Voldemort."
2 "If only our families **didn't** fight all the time."
3 "I wish Lois Lane **knew** who I really was."

> **RULE:** We use *wish / if only* +
> ● We use *wish / if only* + the ¹_____ tense to express how we would like our current situation to be different.
> ● ²_____ to say that we'd like the ability or permission to do something.

> **LOOK!** We can use *was* or *were* after a singular subject (*I, he, she,* or *it*) when we express wishes.
> *I wish I **was** older. / I wish I **were** older.*

2 **Complete the sentences with the correct forms of the verbs.**

see | talk | not get
not be | not fight | have

1 I wish this train trip _____ so long.
2 I wish Liam _____ so much.
3 If only I _____ an interesting book with me.
4 I wish Madison _____ with me all the time.
5 If only Liam _____ so angry with me.
6 If only Madison _____ that I'm in love with her!

3 **SPEAKING** Play "famous wishes" in groups of four.

● Choose a famous fictional person and write three wishes. (Remember: They should be about the present situation, not the past.)

● Read your sentences aloud. The other students have to guess who you are.

Workbook page 37

READING

1 **SPEAKING** Work in pairs. You find a valuable ring in the street. Think of four things you could do with it.

2 Read the story. What did Billy do?

3 Read the story again. Who do you think said these things?

1 "If only a little good luck came my way."
2 "What's that in my cup?"
3 "I'd like to buy it."
4 "It's a lot of money, but I can't."
5 "I was here a few days ago."
6 "I can't believe he didn't sell my ring!"
7 "I think that's a great idea."
8 "We never thought we'd see you again."

4 **SPEAKING** Work in pairs. Imagine this story is going to be made into a Hollywood movie. Discuss these questions.

1 Which actors are you going to choose to play the main characters?
2 How are you going to give the movie a big "Hollywood ending"?
3 What's the title of your movie?

5 Share your ideas with the class.

GRAMMAR
Third conditional

1 Complete these sentences from the story with the correct forms of the verbs. Then complete the rule.

1 If Billy _____ (look) up, he _____ (see) a young lady on her way to work.
2 If he _____ (not do) the right thing, he _____ (not see) his sisters again.

> **RULE:** We use the third conditional to talk about situations and their outcomes in the past. We form it with:
> *if* + 1_____ + 2_____ / would(n't) have + 3_____ .

2 Complete the third conditional sentences.

0 If Billy _had been_ on a different street, Sarah _wouldn't have seen_ him.
1 Sarah _____ (see) the ring if she _____ (look) in the cup.
2 Billy _____ (keep) the ring if Sarah _____ (not return).
3 Sarah _____ (not raise) so much money if she _____ (not put) her story on the Internet.

3 Complete the sentences so that they are true for you.

1 If I hadn't gone to school today, …
2 I'd have been really happy if …
3 If I'd been born 100 years ago, …

Workbook page 37

The day Billy Ray's life changed forever

Billy Ray Harris was homeless. He spent each day on the streets of Kansas City, begging for money for food and maybe a bed for the night. Every day, as he sat thinking about his life, he occasionally heard the sound of a coin or two dropping into his cup. One day, the noise was louder than usual. If Billy had looked up, he'd have seen a young lady on her way to work. But he didn't. A little later, when he looked into the cup, he could hardly believe what he saw. At the bottom was a shining diamond ring.

Billy's first thought was to go straight to a jeweler's, and that's exactly what he did. To his complete amazement, he was offered $4,000. Billy thought long and hard. Was this a mistake? It was more money than he'd seen in a long time. But then he thought about his grandfather, who had brought him up to always do the right thing, and he knew he had to reconsider. His mind was made up. He'd keep the ring, and maybe one day its owner would return.

In fact, he didn't have to wait long. Two days later a young woman approached him while he was begging. She introduced herself as Sarah Darling and asked if he'd found anything unusual in his cup. Billy reached into his pocket and pulled out the ring. When he saw the smile on Sarah's face, he knew he'd made the right decision.

But the story doesn't end there. Sarah told her husband the story and how she wanted to post it on the Internet. He

42

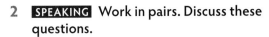

VOCABULARY
Making a decision

1 Read the text below. Then match 1–8 with the underlined words and phrases in the text below.

1	for a long time	☐	5	make	☐
2	a good	☐	6	thought again about	☐
3	the wrong	☐	7	original idea	☐
4	decide	☐	8	made a new decision	☐

My ªfirst thought was to go with the blue. But then I thought ᵇlong and hard and ᶜchanged my mind. Maybe the red was better. But had I made ᵈthe right decision? Had I? I ᵉreconsidered my choice. Red or blue? Red or blue? Why was it so difficult to ᶠmake up my mind? Well, I didn't want to make ᵍa bad decision, did I? So I called my sister. Maybe she could help me ʰcome to a decision.

"Yes, what is it?" she asked.

"Red or blue?" I asked.

"I don't know why you're asking me," she said. "You only ever wear blue."

thought it was a good idea. They also set up an online appeal to raise money for Billy. They soon had more than $185,000.

Billy Ray Harris no longer spends his days begging. He has a home and a job. The story also made the local news, and he was reunited with his two sisters, who he hadn't seen for over 16 years. If he hadn't done the right thing, he wouldn't have seen his sisters again.

2 **SPEAKING** Work in pairs. Discuss these questions.

1 What's the biggest decision you've ever made?

2 Have you ever made the wrong decision? What was it?

3 How good are you at making your mind up about small things?

4 What sort of things do you usually need to think long and hard about?

5 Do you ever reconsider decisions you have made?

6 Who do you ask for help with important decisions?

> Workbook page 38

■ THiNK VALUES ■

Doing the right thing

1 Think about a time when you had to make a difficult decision. Make notes.

1 What decision did you make?

2 What were the consequences?

2 Write a short paragraph. Include a third conditional sentence.

Last year, there was a new student in my class. Nobody wanted to sit next to him, so I did. I'm really happy I did. If I hadn't sat next to him, he wouldn't have become my best friend. What a good decision I made!

3 Read your paragraph aloud to the class. Then vote on the best story.

WRITING
A diary entry about a dilemma

Choose one of these situations or use your own idea. Write a diary entry about it (150–200 words). Try to use language from this unit.

1 Explain the problem.

2 Think about two possible solutions and their consequences.

3 Decide what you're going to do, and why.

- You got in trouble at school. If you tell your parents, you won't be allowed to go to a party.

- Your mom's birthday is this weekend, but you spent all your money on clothes and don't have any left to buy her a present.

- You saw your best friend's boyfriend/girlfriend at the movies with another boy/girl.

And the hole gets deeper!

1 **Look at the photos and answer the questions.**

What is Jeff holding?
Who seems very interested in Mia's friend?

2 🔊 1.27 **Now read and listen to the photostory. Check your answers.**

FLORA What's with the helmet, Jeff?

JEFF It's my dad's. He does go-karting.

MIA Oh, yeah, I remember now. You told us about that. He's pretty good, isn't he?

JEFF Oh, yeah, he's really into it. He goes all the time now that he has his own go-kart. Anyway, there's a problem with his helmet, so he asked me to take it into the shop for him.

MIA Oh, look! There's Chloe.

LEO Who's that?

MIA She's a friend of mine from when I used to be in the orchestra.

JEFF Wow, she's pretty! If I'd known she was in the orchestra, I would have come to more concerts!

CHLOE Hi, Mia. What a nice surprise! How are you?

MIA Good, thanks, Chloe. These are my friends, Leo, Jeff, and Flora.

CHLOE Hi, nice to meet you all. Hey, is that a motorcycle helmet?

JEFF Well, actually, it's a go-kart helmet.

CHLOE So, you're a go-karter? Cool! I've always wanted to try go-karting!

JEFF Well, um, yes. It's just a hobby. But I race, too, you know, now and then. Believe it or not, I've even won a few times.

CHLOE Wow! You actually race. That's so cool. I'd really like to try go-karting, but I've never had the chance.

JEFF Oh, that's a shame. It's a lot of fun.

CHLOE I'm sure it is. Do you think I could …?

JEFF What?

CHLOE Well, I was wondering if I could come along with you sometime, maybe watch you race. Any chance?

JEFF Oh, um, well, maybe. I mean, yes, of course. That would be great.

CHLOE Cool! So, when's your next race?

JEFF Um … Let me think. I'm not sure, to be honest.

CHLOE Well, look, when you know, call me, OK? Mia has my number.

CHLOE Talk to you soon, I hope, Jeff. Bye, everyone!

JEFF Yeah, see you, Chloe.

FLORA Are you out of your mind? You aren't a go-karter, and just now you said you were. Why did you do that?

MIA Do you need to ask?

JEFF Well, she seemed really nice, you know, and she likes go-karting.

LEO Between you and me, I think Jeff has just dug himself into a big hole.

MIA Yes, I think you're right. What are you going to do now, Jeff?

DEVELOPING SPEAKING

3 Work in pairs. Discuss what happens next in the story. Write down your ideas.

We think Jeff asks his dad to help him.

4 ▶ EP2 Watch and find out how the story continues.

5 Mark the sentences T (true) or F (false).

1 Jeff calls Chloe. ☐
2 Chloe asks Jeff if he's really a go-karter. ☐
3 Jeff goes to the go-kart track with his father. ☐
4 Jeff makes a video of himself driving a go-kart. ☐
5 Jeff and Chloe arrange to meet on Sunday. ☐
6 Jeff pretends that he's hurt his knee. ☐
7 His trick is discovered when he uses his phone. ☐
8 Chloe never wants to see Jeff again. ☐

PHRASES FOR FLUENCY

1 Find these expressions in the photostory. Who says them? How do you say them in your language?

1 What's with (the helmet)? _____
2 Believe it or not, … _____
3 I was wondering if … _____
4 Any chance? _____
5 Are you out of your mind? _____
6 Between you and me, … _____

2 Use the expressions in Exercise 1 to complete the conversations.

1 A Andy, _____ you could take my dog Buster for a walk.
  B Sorry, I can't. _____, I'm really scared of dogs.

2 A Hi, Steve. Wow! _____ the really old soccer cleats?
  B I know, they're ancient, aren't they? _____, my dad used to wear them when he was at school. I need new ones.

3 A Hi, Jane. My bike's in the shop and I have to get to the library before it closes. I really need to borrow your bike. _____?
  B _____? It's brand new! I wouldn't lend it to anyone!

Pronunciation
Consonant–vowel word linking
Go to page 120. 🔊

WordWise
now

1 Look at the words and phrases in bold in these sentences from the photostory. Match them with the definitions.

1 Oh yeah, I remember **now**. ☐
2 He goes all the time **now that** he has his own go-kart. ☐
3 But I race, too, you know, **now and then**. ☐
4 You aren't a go-karter, and **just now** you said you were. ☐
5 What are you going to do **now**, Jeff? ☐

a in the near future
b at this moment
c a moment or two ago
d because finally
e sometimes

2 Use words and phrases from Exercise 1 to complete the sentences.

1 I've finished my work, so _____ I'm going to hang out with my friends.
2 I don't listen to this music all the time, but I like to play it _____.
3 Sally was here _____, but she's left.
4 I'll eat later. I'm not hungry _____.
5 I drive to school _____ I have a car.

Workbook page 38

FUNCTIONS
Apologizing and accepting apologies

1 Put the expressions in the correct columns.

No problem. | I'm so sorry. | I feel awful about this. That's/It's OK. | I don't know what to say. Don't worry about it. | No worries. | I'm so ashamed.

Apologizing	Accepting apologies

2 Work in pairs. Imagine you're in these situations and act out conversations. Use expressions from Exercise 1.

- A has spilled a drink on B's pants.
- A has arrived very late for a meeting with B.
- A has bumped into B, and B has fallen down.
- A has completely forgotten B's name.

45

THiNK EXAMS

LISTENING
Part 1: Multiple choice

Workbook page 35

1 ◀))1.30 **You will hear people talking in eight different situations. For questions 1–8, choose the best answer (A, B, or C).**

1 You hear a boy talking about how he got his name. Why was it hard for his parents to name him?
A They each wanted different names.
B There weren't many possibilities for a name that worked in two languages.
C He was born two weeks early.

2 You hear a girl talking on her phone. What is her problem?
A She doesn't want to invite Lucy to her birthday celebration.
B Her mom said that Lucy can't come for a sleepover.
C She really wants to have a big party.

3 You hear part of an interview with a soccer player. What does he find most difficult about his job?
A not being free on weekends
B having to work out every day
C the comments some of the fans make

4 You hear two friends talking about a camping trip. What advice does Alan give Steve?
A to take a comfortable sleeping bag
B to get a ride to the campsite
C not to take things that weigh too much

5 You hear a local news report. What did Chuck Roberts think when he found the money?
A I'm $10,000 richer.
B How can I return this to the owner?
C Could I keep this? Would anybody ever know?

6 Two friends are talking about a party. Why did Chloe miss the party?
A Her dad said she had to go biking with him.
B She fell asleep in the middle of the day.
C She was watching TV and forgot the time.

7 You hear a girl talking about a difficult decision. Why did she find it hard to choose which classes to take?
A She had no idea about what career she wanted to have.
B She didn't want to disappoint her dad.
C She wanted to make sure her classes would help her get a well-paid job.

8 You hear a book review on the radio. What did Carla like most about the book?
A that she was able to understand the story
B that it was a love story
C the way the romance developed during the story

WRITING
Part 2: Story

Workbook page 43

2 **Your English teacher has asked you to write a short story for the school's new website. The story must begin or end with the following words:**

That name! Why did my parents give me that stupid name?!

Write your story in 140–190 words.

VOCABULARY

1 Complete the sentences with the words / phrases in the list. There are four extra words / phrases.

brand | call | chain | cheat | consumers | get away with | image
logo | manufacturer | make | name | own up to | products | tell

1 She worked very hard for years to _____ a name for herself in the theater.
2 The company was in trouble until they started making some new _____.
3 If you _____ during the test, we'll take you out of the room and destroy your paper.
4 I like so many different kinds of music. Basically, you _____ it, I like it!
5 He tried to look at another boy's test, but the teacher saw him, so he didn't _____ it.
6 I think it's so childish when you _____ other people names.
7 We didn't like our old _____ so we got a new one designed. It's on our website now.
8 Did you eat the last piece of apple pie? Come on – _____ me the truth!
9 We started with just one store, but now we have a _____ of twenty.
10 I know you took my things without asking. Why don't you just _____ it? **/10**

GRAMMAR

2 Complete the sentences with the words in the list. There are two extra words.

better | if | go | ought | unless | until | went | when

1 It's pretty late. I think I have to _____ now, OK?
2 I really wish we _____ out to eat more often.
3 I'll call you _____ the movie ends, OK?
4 I'm not going to bed _____ I finish this book – it's amazing!
5 You'll never be his friend _____ you go and talk to him!
6 It's a secret, so you'd _____ not tell anyone else!

3 Find and correct the mistake in each sentence.

1 You shouldn't to talk to me like that. It isn't nice. _____
2 If they wouldn't be so mean, I'd invite them to my party. _____
3 I wish you don't live so far away. _____
4 Your eye looks bad. I think you better go to the doctor. _____
5 If it hadn't rained, we had gone to the beach yesterday. _____
6 If only we can see you more often. _____ **/12**

FUNCTIONAL LANGUAGE

4 Circle the correct words.

1 A I think we *should / ought* to go now.
  B That's a shame. If only you *could stay / stayed* a little longer.
2 A Listen, *we must not / we don't have to* miss the train tomorrow morning.
  B You're right. *I'd better not / I don't have to* forget to set the alarm on my phone.
3 A Hey! Stop! You *don't / can't* come in here. You're too young!
  B Sorry! But I really want to see the movie. I wish I *would be / were* 18 already! **/8**
4 A Patrick *wouldn't have / won't have* come to the party if he'd known
     Sue was going to be there.
  B Yeah, it's a shame – if only *we'd told / we've told* him earlier.

MY SCORE **/30**

| 22 – 30 |
| 10 – 21 |
| 0 – 9 |

5 WHAT A STORY!

OBJECTIVES

FUNCTIONS: telling a story
GRAMMAR: relative pronouns; defining and non-defining relative clauses; relative clauses with *which*
VOCABULARY: types of stories; elements of a story

READING

1 **Think of an example of each of these things.**

- a story or a favorite fairy tale from your childhood
- a favorite movie
- a thriller (either a book or a movie) that really grabbed you
- an anecdote or a joke you've heard recently

2 **SPEAKING** Work in pairs. Share one or two of your ideas from Exercise 1.

3 **SPEAKING** Why do you think people like stories so much? With a partner, discuss as many reasons as you can think of. Then compare your ideas with the rest of the class.

4 **◄)) 1.31** Read and listen to the article. Were your ideas the same as the writer's?

5 **Read the article again. Answer the questions using evidence from the text.**

1 What examples does the writer give to show that storytelling is popular in the modern world?

2 What point is the writer making in paragraph 2?

3 What did the Neanderthal man *not* want to do when telling the story?

4 How did storytellers manage to keep people interested in their stories over the years?

5 How have storytellers contributed to society in different cultures?

6 Why can stories be very important for a country and its culture?

■ TRAIN TO THiNK ■

Thinking about different writing styles

Writers use different techniques to bring their texts alive.

6 **Answer the questions.**

1 What technique does the writer use in the title of the article?

2 How many times does he use this technique in the article?

3 Why do you think he does this?

7 **Choose the correct option.**

1 When people ask a rhetorical question, they …
   A expect an answer.
   B don't really expect an answer.

2 They ask a rhetorical question to …
   A introduce a subject they want to talk about.
   B find out what you're thinking.

8 **Paragraphs 4 and 5 don't contain any rhetorical questions. Think of a rhetorical question that you could add to each paragraph.**

Everybody loves stories – but why?

What's the first image that comes to mind when you hear the word "storytelling"? A parent who's reading a fairy tale to a little child – that's what most of us think of immediately. But there's more to stories than fairy tales. What about our favorite movies, the thriller you're reading right now, and that friend who's so great at telling jokes and anecdotes? The movies, the thrillers, the anecdotes, and the jokes: They all have something in common with fairy tales. They're all based on the same activity, which is one of the most fascinating and unique accomplishments of the human race: telling stories!

But why do we tell stories? Just for fun? Here's a story for you. Imagine the world fifty thousand years ago. A group of people are sitting around the fire in a cave, where they've just finished eating a big meal together. One of them has an idea. He wants to get some berries, which he wants to share with everybody. His friend decides to join him.

Off they go, out of the cave, down to the place where the best berries grow. They don't come back for a long while. Finally, the only one of them to return is the friend, who is covered in blood. He tells the others that as soon as they went around the bend, not far from the cave, a saber-toothed cat attacked them and killed his friend. The listeners are shocked, of course, but they're also warned.

Are you getting the idea? Stories aren't just about entertainment. They contain messages, which might be useful for us in the future, like the cave man's story, which certainly wasn't intended to entertain his friends! Good stories engage us emotionally, and they do that by giving us something to think about.

We admire people whose magical storytelling skills capture our attention and our imagination. Throughout human history storytellers have been important and respected members of society. In the past, storytellers often traveled a lot. When they went to places far away, their stories traveled with them. When they returned home, they had new stories to share. People were eager to listen, which was fun but also gave them a chance to learn about those remote places.

In cultures all over the world, important stories are passed down. They come from previous generations, whose wisdom and knowledge they contain. They're often about disasters, dramatic events such as fires, storms, thunder, lightning, and floods. Every country and culture has its own stories. Our stories have become part of our tradition. Our stories reflect who we are.

SPEAKING

Work in pairs. Discuss these questions.

1 What kind of stories do you enjoy most? Give an example.
2 Have you ever told someone a story that your parents or grandparents told you? Where did they hear the story?

GRAMMAR
Relative pronouns

1 **Complete these sentences from the article on page 49. Then complete the rule.**

1 A group of Neanderthals are sitting around the fire in a cave, _____ they've just finished eating a big meal together.

2 He wants to get some berries, _____ he wants to share with everybody.

3 What about that friend _____'s great at telling jokes and anecdotes?

4 They come from previous generations, _____ wisdom and knowledge they contain.

> **RULE:** We use relative clauses to give extra information. We use …
>
> 1 _____ to refer to people.
>
> 2 _____ and _____ to refer to things.
>
> 3 _____ and _____ to refer to possessions.
>
> 4 _____ and _____ to refer to places.

2 **In your notebook, combine the sentences by replacing the underlined words with relative pronouns from Exercise 1.**

1 One of the world's greatest storytellers is Stephen King. He has sold more than 400 million books.

2 Many people love his horror stories. The horror stories are often quite shocking.

3 The best storyteller I know is my uncle. He lived in India for several years.

4 We love listening to our English teacher. Her stories are fascinating.

5 At our school we have a great library. We like to relax and read there.

Workbook page 46

Defining and non-defining relative clauses

3 **Complete these sentences from the article on page 49. Then read the rule.**

1 What's the first image _____ comes to mind when you hear the word "storytelling"?

2 A parent _____'s reading a fairy tale to a little child.

3 Off they go, out of the cave, down to the place _____ the best berries grow.

4 The only one of them to return is the friend, _____'s covered in blood.

5 We admire people _____ magical storytelling skills capture our imagination.

> **RULE:** We use a **defining relative clause** to identify an object, a person, a place, or a possession. Without this information, it's hard to know who or what we're talking about.
> *The man was angry.* (Which man?)
> *The man **whose bag had been stolen** was angry.*
>
> We use a **non-defining relative clause** to add extra information. We don't need this information to understand the sentence. We put commas around it.
> *Stephen King is a famous writer.*
> *Stephen King, who is American, is a famous writer.*
> (Extra information: He's American.)

4 **Complete these defining relative clauses with *who*, *where*, *whose*, or *that*.**

1 The house _____ I grew up is next to a school.

2 A book _____ has lots of short chapters is perfect for the bus ride to school.

3 A person _____ knows a lot of jokes is usually a good public speaker.

4 We went to a lecture by a writer _____ books are always on the best-seller list.

5 The author _____ wrote the famous teen novel *The Outsiders* was only 16.

5 **Check (✓) the sentences that contain non-defining relative clauses and add commas.**

1 My brother is someone who just doesn't like fantasy novels. ☐

2 Fairy tales which were written for children are now being adapted for the movies. ☐

3 The Brothers Grimm whose stories have fascinated millions of children lived in the 19th century. ☐

4 It's difficult to read in places where people are talking on cell phones. ☐

Workbook page 46

VOCABULARY
Types of stories

1 🔊 1.32 Match the types of story with the book covers. Write numbers 1–9 in the boxes. Then listen and check.

1 mystery novel
2 science fiction novel
3 historical novel
4 horror story
5 (auto)biography
6 short stories
7 romantic novel
8 travel literature
9 poetry

2 Which are nonfiction?

3 **SPEAKING** Which types of literature do you like reading most? ▸ Workbook page 48 ▸

SPEAKING

1 Work in pairs. If you had to choose one of the books in the previous exercise, which would it be, and why?

> *I'd choose … because the cover looks / the title sounds (exciting / funny / interesting / …).*

2 Prepare a one-minute talk about reading. Think about the following points and take notes.
- what you prefer: articles, short stories, novels, etc.
- where and when you like reading

3 Take turns giving your talks in small groups.

LISTENING

1 Find out how much your class knows about Stephen King. Then read the biographical data.

Stephen King: fact file

- King was born in 1947 in Portland, Maine.
- He wanted to be a teacher but couldn't get a job. He worked in a laundry and did various other jobs while continuing to write stories.
- He published his first book, *Carrie*, in 1974. It became a huge success.
- He's written about 50 novels and over 200 horror, fantasy, and science fiction short stories. Many of them have been made into movies.

2 🔊 1.33 Listen to two teenagers talking about a short story by Stephen King called *Word Processor of the Gods*. What's the last word displayed on the computer screen?

3 🔊 1.33 Listen again and make notes to answer the questions.

1 What has the man always wanted to have? Why?
2 What kind of relationship does he have with his son and his nephew?
3 What event makes the man very unhappy?
4 What happens when he goes to his shed the next day?
5 Why does he get angry? What does he do next?
6 What happens in the end?

4 **SPEAKING** Compare your answers in pairs.

▮ THiNK SELF-ESTEEM ▮
A better world

SPEAKING Think about these questions. Make notes. Then compare your ideas in class.

1 Imagine you had a machine like the one in the story. If you could eliminate one problem in the world, what would it be? Why?

2 If you could use the machine to create something to make the world a better place, what sentence would you type in?

READING

1   Look at the photos. Do you recognize these fairy tales? Do you know their names in English?

2   Read the article quickly. Who wrote some of these stories?

Hollywood fairy tales

Little Red Riding Hood used to be just a story that parents read to their children at bedtime. Now *Red Riding Hood* is a Hollywood blockbuster directed by Catherine Hardwicke. Hardwicke directed *Twilight*, which made her the obvious choice for another movie so clearly aimed at the teenage market.

Red Riding Hood isn't the only movie to go back to the classic fairy tales and update them for today's teenagers. *Hansel and Gretel: Witch Hunters*, *Jack the Giant Slayer*, and *Snow White and the Huntsman* are also hoping they can persuade young people to revisit the stories of their childhood. And then there's *The Brothers Grimm*, starring Matt Damon and Heath Ledger, which saw the original authors of many of these fairy tales come face to face with some of their characters. Hollywood has realized that fairy tales have the potential to make money, and lots of it.

Teenagers are one of Hollywood's most important markets. After the success of series like *Harry Potter*, *Twilight*, and more recently, *The Hunger Games*, movie studios are looking for more inspiration for stories to keep young people returning to the theaters. Fairy tales might just be the answer. Many are already very dark, which makes them ideal for adolescents, who are often fascinated by that side of life. Of course, you might not recognize much of the original story, as extra horror and romance for the heroes and heroines have been added to the plots. But with modern-day special effects to bring it all to life, these ancient stories are new again.

3   Read the article again and connect the sentences.

1   Catherine Hardwicke has made
2   Several movies have been produced
3   *The Brothers Grimm* shows how the
4   Movies based on fairy tales have
5   Teenagers are often interested
6   When you compare the movies to

famous writers meet the heroes
turned out to be extremely
the stories they are based on,
in characters that are evil,
a name for herself as a director
that remind young people of the

stories they enjoyed as children.
you will notice big differences.
of movies for a teen audience.
successful commercially.
and villains of their stories.
angry, or unhappy.

4   **SPEAKING** Work in pairs. Discuss these questions.

1   What fairy tales are popular in your country?

2   Do you agree that many teenagers are interested in the "dark" side of life? Why? / Why not?

WRITING
A fairy tale

Think of a fairy tale and write the story (200 words). Think about:

*   the ordering of the story.
*   how to use a good selection of past tenses.
*   how to bring the story alive with adjectives and adverbs.

Don't forget: fairy tales start with *Once upon a time* ....

GRAMMAR
Relative clauses with *which*

1 Complete these sentences from the article on page 52. Add commas where necessary. What does *which* refer to in each of the sentences? Complete the rule.

1 Hardwicke directed *Twilight* _____ made her the obvious choice for another movie so clearly aimed at the teenage market.

2 Many [fairy tales] are already very dark _____ makes them ideal for adolescents.

> **RULE:** The pronoun [1]_____ normally refers to a noun, but it can sometimes refer to all of the previous clause.
>
> We cannot use [2]_____ or *that* in the same way.
>
> *She was late, **which** made her nervous.*
> NOT ~~She was late, **what / that** made her nervous.~~

2 In your notebook, join the pairs of sentences as shown using *which*.

0 I often play the drums on Sunday mornings. This annoys the neighbors.

I often play *the drums on Sunday mornings, which annoys* the neighbors.

1 She's lost all her money. This means she'll be in trouble.

She's lost … in trouble.

2 Nobody in class learned the new words. It was frustrating for our teacher.

Nobody in class … for our teacher.

3 Fairy tales have been turned into successful teen movies. This has surprised many people.

Fairy tales … many people.

4 It's really amazing that Stephen King manages to write several books per year.

Stephen King … really amazing.

5 It's fascinating that almost all of his books have been made into movies.

Almost all of his books … fascinating.

3 Complete the sentences so that they are true for you.

0 My favorite singer *is giving a concert in our town next month*, which is fantastic.

1 … last year, which made me feel really proud.

2 I heard on the news …, which I was really upset about.

3 …, which really isn't easy.

4 **SPEAKING** Work in pairs. Share your sentences. How long can you keep each conversation going?

> *My favorite singer is giving a concert in our town next month, which is fantastic.*
>
> *Really? Who's that?*
>
> *Lorde.*
>
> *Wow! I like her songs, too. Do you know when …?*

Workbook page 47

VOCABULARY
Elements of a story

1 Match the words with their definitions.

plot | setting | hero | character
opening | ending | villain | dialogue

1 the story of a movie, play, etc. _____

2 a person in a story _____

3 the last part of a story _____

4 the main (good) character in a story _____

5 a character who harms other people _____

6 the words that the characters say to each other _____

7 the beginning of a story _____

8 the time and place in which the action happens _____

2 Think about these things for two minutes. Make notes.

- a movie or book with a great plot
- the setting of the last movie you saw
- a movie with a great opening
- a good movie with a disappointing ending
- an actor who's really good at playing villains

3 **SPEAKING** Work in pairs or small groups. Share your ideas.

Workbook page 48

Culture

1 **Look at the photos and answer the questions.**

1 What can you see in the photos?
2 What do you think the person is doing?
3 Would you like to visit this place? Why or why not?

2 🔊 **1.34** **Read and listen to the article. Check your answers.**

IRELAND

A nation of storytellers

Hardly any country can claim to have a richer storytelling tradition than Ireland. This is the result of a mixture of many people – the Celts, the Vikings, the Normans, and the English – who came to the island at various times and all left a little of their culture behind.

In the Celtic tradition of spoken storytelling, singers and poets called bards were extremely important people. Before there was written language, bards had to memorize the stories, poems, and songs to be able to perform them live. Storytellers used to move from village to village. Wherever they appeared, they were warmly welcomed, and people gave them food and shelter for the night.

Good storytellers knew hundreds of stories by heart. The stories were the only record of important events, and people appreciated them: They were the best entertainment available. This tradition has been influential for more than 2,000 years, and in many ways, it's still alive today. Stories have been handed down from generation to generation, with very little change.

The Irish love of stories can be felt all over the country. In many places, older people still remember the *céilí* (pronounced KAY-lee and meaning "get-together"), in which people would meet in a house, sit near the fire, tell stories, sing songs, dance, and play music. Interestingly, in recent years, there have been successful attempts to revive this tradition, and some of the most popular contemporary storytellers are very young.

The elegant way talented storytellers use language is called "the gift of the gab." If you want to get the gift of the gab, you have to go to Blarney Castle in Cork. You have to climb to the top of the castle, lie down, and bend over backwards to kiss the Stone of Eloquence. And, of course, there's a story to explain this. It tells of an Irish king who rescued a woman when she fell into a river. The woman was so grateful that she cast a spell over him. She gave him the ability to speak so well that he could persuade people to do whatever he wanted. But, for the spell to work, he had to kiss a particular stone on top of Blarney Castle. This is what he did, and it worked. So whoever kisses the Blarney Stone will get the same gift.

You don't believe in such stories? Well, it's true, and you can easily prove it. Just climb to the top of Blarney Castle and kiss that stone …

3 **Read the article again. Mark the sentences T (true) or F (false).**

1 Irish culture has several different influences. ☐
2 Bards used to write down their stories and poems. ☐
3 Irish storytellers were often given hospitality in return for telling stories. ☐
4 It's no longer possible to go to a *céilí*. ☐
5 If people have "the gift of the gab," they're good at telling stories. ☐

4 **SPEAKING** **Work in pairs. Discuss these questions.**

1 How does the Irish storytelling tradition compare with storytelling in your country?
2 What stories are there about places near where you live?

5 VOCABULARY There are eight highlighted words or phrases in the text. Match them with these definitions.

1 passed (from older people to younger people) _____

2 change the position of your body so your head is nearer the floor _____

3 were able to say from memory _____

4 bring back to life _____

5 document _____

6 said words that had magical powers _____

7 gave value or importance to _____

8 a safe place to stay _____

SPEAKING

1 Look at the pictures. Put them in order and use them to tell a story.

2 🔊 1.35 Listen and compare your story to the one you hear.

FUNCTIONS
Telling a story

1 🔊 1.35 Annie uses these expressions to bring her story to life. Match them with the correct places in the conversation. Then listen again and check.

☐ you'll never believe what

☐ The strangest thing happened to me the other day.

☐ Well, let me finish.

☐ That was the annoying thing.

☐ What are the chances?

ANNIE ¹_____

JACK What?

ANNIE I woke up with this song in my head, and I couldn't stop singing it all day long. It was really annoying.

JACK What was it?

ANNIE ²_____ It was a song I knew, but I couldn't remember what it was. I even sang it to a few of my friends, but they didn't know what it was either.

JACK So what was so strange about that?

ANNIE ³_____ I got home from school (with the song still in my head), and I went upstairs to do my homework. I decided to turn on the radio to try to forget the song, and ⁴_____ they were playing!

JACK What?

ANNIE They were playing the song that I'd been singing all day!

JACK So you were singing a song from the radio, but you'd forgotten the name of it.

ANNIE Yes, but the strange thing is that it wasn't a song from now. It was some obscure song from the 1980s that you never hear anymore. It was a song that my dad used to play when I was really little. I hadn't heard it in years. And they were playing it on the radio! ⁵_____

JACK Yes, that is pretty weird.

2 Think of a strange story that happened to you or to someone else.

- Write down the main events in note form.
- Think how you can use some of the expressions.
- In groups, tell your stories.

Pronunciation

/ə/ in word endings

Go to page 120. 🔊

6 | HOW DO THEY DO IT?

OBJECTIVES

FUNCTIONS: talking about sequence; explaining how things are done

GRAMMAR: present and past passive (review); *have something done*; future and present perfect passive

VOCABULARY: extreme adjectives and modifiers; *make* and *do*

READING

1 **SPEAKING** Work in pairs. Discuss these questions.

1 What magicians can you name?
2 What magic tricks have you seen?
3 Can you do any tricks yourself? What are they?

2 Read and listen to the article about Dynamo. Which four of his tricks does it mention?

3 ◀)) 1.38 Read the article again and match
✳ sentences a–g with spaces 1–6. There's one extra sentence. Then listen and check.

- [ ] a He won a few local and national Magic Circle championships.
- [ ] b This wasn't the first time Dynamo had amazed the people of London.
- [ ] c The man was walking on water!
- [ ] d Was he going to throw himself in?
- [ ] e His grandfather was a talented amateur magician and taught Stephen many of his tricks.
- [ ] f Dynamo refuses to tell anyone how he does his tricks.
- [ ] g Was he really walking on air?

■ TRAIN TO THiNK ■

Understanding what's relevant

To write a good text, a writer must make sure that each sentence is linked to what comes before it. Understanding how this is done will help you to do tasks like Exercise 3.

4 Choose the sentence that *doesn't* have any relevance to the first.

Dynamo has a TV show.
A Lots of famous guests appear on it.
B TV is popular with teens all over the world.
C It's been running for three years now.

5 Work in pairs. Use this sentence to make a similar task for your partner.

Dynamo has amazed the people of London twice.
A _____
B _____
C _____

The man who walks on air

One Saturday afternoon in June, in the busy streets of central London, something strange happened. A man was seen apparently floating beside a London bus as it drove around town. One of his arms was stretched out and was attached to the roof of the bus. This arm appeared to be the only thing supporting the rest of his body. The man waved to the crowds with his other hand and moved his legs. [1]_____ How was it possible? It turned out to be the latest illusion from Dynamo, one of the world's most thrilling illusionists and the star of his own TV show, *Dynamo: Magician Impossible*.

[2]_____ Two years earlier, tourists walking by the River Thames were a little concerned to see a young man go down some steps to the edge of the freezing cold river and look thoughtfully across to the other side. [3]_____ More and more people gathered on the bridge to see what was going on. And then, to their complete disbelief, he lifted up his foot and stepped onto the water. He didn't sink! Then he took another step, and another, and another.

[4]_____ A few minutes later, when the man was a quarter of the way across the river, a police boat arrived. The man was pulled into the boat and they sped away, leaving a huge crowd of amazed spectators. Of course, hundreds of photos were taken by onlookers, and the next day newspapers were full of the fascinating story.

Dynamo is the stage name of Stephen Frayne, who was born in the northern English town of Bradford. [5]_____ As a child, Stephen visited New Orleans and saw street magicians for the first time. It was then that Stephen knew he wanted to be a magician when he grew up. He started off learning card tricks and later combined them with a little breakdancing to create an original act. He was soon making a name for himself.

[6]_____ A TV show quickly followed and featured celebrities including Dizzee Rascal, Ms. Dynamite, Will Smith, and One Direction. As his famous guests watched, Dynamo performed tricks like turning a five-pound note into £20 and turning paper butterflies into real ones. But what everyone wants to know now is, after walking on air and walking on water, what is he going to do next?

So how is it done?

Most people agree that the bus illusion involves a fake arm with a metal pole running through it. This arm is attached to the bus and is used to support Dynamo's body. The walking on water illusion is more difficult to explain. Some people think he walks on glass boards that are put in the water before. Others say he's attached by invisible ropes to camouflaged helicopters that fly high above. What do you think?

SPEAKING

Work in pairs. Discuss these questions.

1 How do you think Dynamo walked on water?
2 Why do you think people enjoy magic tricks so much?

Pronunciation

The /ʒ/ phoneme
Go to page 120.

GRAMMAR
Present and past passive (review)

1 **Complete these sentences from the article on page 57. Use the correct form of *be*. Then complete the rule with *by*, *be*, and *past participle*.**

1 The man _____ pulled into the boat …

2 Of course, hundreds of photos _____ taken by onlookers …

3 This arm _____ attached to the bus and _____ used to support Dynamo's body.

4 Some people think he walks on glass boards that _____ put in the water before.

> **RULE:** We form the passive with a form of the verb
> [1]_____ and the [2]_____.
> We use the preposition [3]_____ to say who or what does the action, but only if this is important.

2 **Complete the instructions for this trick with the correct active or passive forms of the verbs.**

~~use~~ | cut | hold | pull | get | push | hide

0 A long box *is used* for this trick.

1 One woman _____ at one end of the box.

2 A second woman _____ into the box.

3 She puts her head out of one end and _____ her legs to her chest with her arms. At the same time, the first woman _____ her legs out of the other end.

4 The box _____ in half by the magician.

5 The ends of the box _____ apart to show that it has been cut in two.

Workbook page 54

VOCABULARY
Extreme adjectives and modifiers

1 **Look at these phrases from the article on page 57. What do the adjectives in bold mean?**

1 one of the world's most **thrilling** illusionists

2 a **huge** crowd of amazed spectators

3 the edge of the **freezing** river

4 newspapers were full of the **fascinating** story

2 **Match the gradable adjectives 1–5 with the extreme adjectives a–e.**

1	good		a	hilarious
2	funny		b	delighted
3	happy		c	huge / enormous
4	big		d	tiny / minute
5	small		e	great / fantastic / amazing / awesome / wonderful

> **LOOK!** We use:
> • *very* with gradable adjectives.
> • *absolutely* with extreme adjectives.
> • *really* with gradable and extreme adjectives.

3 **Look at these examples of adjectives with the modifiers *very*, *really*, and *absolutely*. Which combinations are correct and which are incorrect? Mark them ✓ or ✗.**

1 really good

2 really amazing

3 very funny

4 very hilarious

5 absolutely small

6 absolutely tiny

4 **Complete the text with adjectives from Exercise 2. Sometimes more than one answer is possible, but don't use each adjective more than once.**

> Last night we went to a magic show. It was very good – in fact, it was absolutely [1]_____. The magician was really [2]_____ – we couldn't stop laughing. In one trick, he had two hats: a really small one and an [3]_____ one. But from the big hat he pulled out an absolutely [4]_____ rabbit and from the small hat he pulled out a huge one. It was so much fun and I left feeling really [5]_____.

Workbook page 56

LISTENING

1 ◁)) 1.41 **Listen to two people talking about a tattoo. Which animal does Dave's tattoo show?**

2 ◁)) 1.41 **Listen again. Check (✓) the reasons why Kim is so upset about Dave's tattoo.**

1 She knows his parents will be angry. ☐

2 She thinks it looks terrible. ☐

3 She thinks it was too expensive. ☐

4 She thinks his brother will want to get one, too. ☐

5 She thinks he's too young to have a tattoo. ☐

3 **Who says these lines, Kim or Dave? What is the context? Complete the table in your notebook.**

Who?	What?	Why?
Kim	What?! You … You …	She's so shocked at Dave's tattoo that she can't speak.
	So, do you like it?	
	Whatever. I like it.	
	I'm going to kill you!	

GRAMMAR

have something done

1 <u>Underline</u> **the subject in each sentence. Do we know who is performing the action? Then complete the rule with *us* and *someone*.**

1 I've had my arm tattooed.

2 I can have it removed.

3 I'm going to have my hair dyed.

> **RULE:** We often use the structure *have* + object + past participle when we arrange for ¹_____ to do something for ²_____. In less formal contexts, *get* often replaces *have*.

2 **Complete the sentences. Use *have* + object + past participle.**

Lord Layabout doesn't do anything himself.

1 He never cooks. He _____ his meals _____ by chefs.

2 He and his wife never do any housework. They _____ it _____ by housekeepers.

3 He never goes to stores. He _____ everything _____ by his assistant.

4 Neither he nor his wife drives. They _____ their car _____ by an ex-racing driver.

5 They never plan parties. They _____ them _____ by party planners.

6 They don't take care of their children. They _____ them _____ by a nanny.

3 **In your notebook, use these words to write questions for each answer.**

~~hair~~ | wedding cake | car | eyes | teeth
check | repair | make | ~~cut~~ | clean

0 At the To Dye For salon.
Where can you have your hair cut?

1 At Derek's Bakery.

2 At Bridge Street Garage.

3 At City Vision.

4 At the Northgate Dental Clinic.

Workbook page 54 ➤

▌THiNK SELF-ESTEEM ▌

Life changes

1 **Match the photos with 1–4.**

1 "My parents won't let me get my hair dyed."

2 "What a bad idea it was to get a tattoo!"

3 "I'm not allowed to have my ears pierced."

4 "It'd be cool to have my head shaved, but Dad wouldn't like it."

2 **SPEAKING** **Work in pairs. Think of three reasons the parents of these teenagers might give for their disapproval.**

3 **SPEAKING** **What are your feelings about these issues? Tell your partner.**

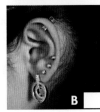

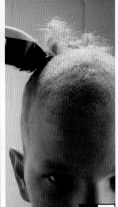

READING

1 Read the article and number the photos in the order that they are mentioned.

 A
 B
 C
 D
 E
 F

How Do They Do That?

I've just discovered a fantastic new show called *How Do They Do That?* It's one of the best shows on TV right now! The idea is simple: Take a topic – like travel, for example – and then think of lots of little mysteries that could be explained. How do planes take off and land? How do driverless cars work? How do they build model boats in a bottle? That sort of thing. Then get two young, enthusiastic hosts, dress them in white coats, and put them in a laboratory to do lots of exciting experiments. Add some cool graphics to explain the rest and there's your show. Get the idea?

Each episode looks at a different subject. As well as travel, topics that have already been covered include education, the body, things around the house, and magic – my favorite so far. Still to come are personal finances, the natural world, sports, and life and how to live it.

What I like most about the show is that it's fun and you learn something at the same time, so you don't feel so guilty about spending 60 minutes in front of the TV each week. We've been shown how to boil the perfect egg (wash it, put it in boiling water for three minutes, and then leave it in the water for an additional 60 seconds); how birds make their way back to exactly the same place each summer (they use the stars); and how a touchscreen works (that one didn't really make much sense to me). We haven't been shown how to eat chocolate without putting on weight yet, but I'm still hoping they might include that!

In future episodes, secrets such as how Usain Bolt can run so fast and how spiders make webs will be revealed. The one I'm personally looking forward to the most is how to meet the perfect partner.

So if you aren't already watching *How Do They Do That?*, I strongly recommend that you make the time. It gives you facts that you can use to pretend that you're actually really intelligent – as long as you can remember them, of course. It's on every Tuesday at 9 p.m., but this week's episode won't be shown until half an hour later because of the live international soccer game. Get watching and start learning!

2 Read the article again. Answer the questions.

1 What do the hosts wear on *How Do They Do That?* Why do you think they do this?

2 How many different episodes are mentioned?

3 What's the best way to cook an egg?

4 Why couldn't the writer tell you how a touchscreen works?

5 What evidence is there that the writer doesn't have a partner?

6 What time will this week's episode start?

3 In which episode are these questions probably answered?

1 How do you buy a house?

2 How do you do well on a test?

3 How do you do the housework in half an hour?

4 How do whales communicate?

5 How does a GPS work?

4 **SPEAKING** Work in pairs. Choose four of the episodes and think of a question you would like to have answered in each one.

GRAMMAR
Future and present perfect passive

1 **Complete the sentences from the article on page 60 with the words in the list. Then complete the rule with** *past participle* **(x2),** *be,* **and** *present perfect.*

been shown | been covered
be shown | be revealed

1 … topics that have already _____ include education …

2 We haven't _____ how to eat chocolate without putting on weight yet …

3 In future episodes, secrets such as how Usain Bolt can run so fast […] will _____ .

4 … but this week's episode won't _____ until half an hour later …

> **RULE:**
> - To make the future passive, we use *will* +
>   ¹_____ + the ²_____ .
> - To make the present perfect passive, we use the ³_____ form of *be* and the ⁴_____ .

2 **Rewrite the sentences in your notebook using the passive voice.**

1 They will show the game live on TV.
2 They will choose the next Olympic city in April.
3 They have already sold all the tickets for the show.
4 Someone has already spent that money.

3 **Complete the text with the future passive form of the verbs.**

Good news for fans of *How Do They Do That?*
New episodes ¹_____ (film)
in the summer, and the new shows
²_____ (air) in the new year. The
shows ³_____ (host) by Helen, but
she ⁴_____ (not join) by Liam this
time. A new host ⁵_____ (choose)
in the next week – watch this space! The hosts
⁶_____ also _____ (join) by Spike
the robot dog! Topics that ⁷_____
(cover) include buildings, space, and food.
There'll also be a new time for the show. It
⁸_____ (not show) at the old time
of 9 p.m. on Tuesdays. It ⁹_____
(move) to Sunday afternoons at 3 p.m., and the
producers are hoping it ¹⁰_____
(watch) by a bigger audience.

4 **Look at the list and write sentences. Use affirmative and negative present perfect passive forms and** *already* **or** *yet.*

Mom and Dad's anniversary party —

choose a date for the party ✔
buy decorations ✗
find a place for the party ✔
send invitations ✔
buy drinks ✗
prepare food ✗
hire a DJ ✔
choose music ✗

A date has already been chosen for the party.
The decorations haven't been bought yet.

Workbook page 55

VOCABULARY
make and *do*

1 **Write the words in the correct columns. Use page 60 to help you.**

an experiment | your way | sense
time | money | well | housework

make	do

2 **Complete the sentences with the correct form of** *make* **or** *do.*

0 I really need to ___*do*___ well on this test. I'm going to study hard tonight.

1 I've been _____ housework all day. I'm exhausted.

2 There's a really good exhibit at the museum right now. You should _____ time to see it.

3 Sorry I can't meet you at the station. You'll have to _____ your own way to my house.

4 Don't go in there. They're _____ a dangerous experiment.

5 The movie is very long, so it _____ sense to have something to eat first.

6 He _____ a lot of money in his career and retired when he was 50.

Workbook page 56

Fiction

1 **What is a "mind map"? What do people use them for?**

2 **▶ 2.02 Read and listen to the extract. Answer the questions.**

1 What is the connection between the mind map and the pendant?
2 What kind of book do you think *The Mind Map* is?

friends

sense

make

a cake

time

a noise

The Mind Map by David Morrison

Lucho has always found homework boring. But when he draws a mind map to plan an essay on stolen gold, something very strange happens. The mind map is trying to tell him something. But what is it?

Eva was sitting on the grass with her back to the library, reading her history textbook. Lucho tried to walk slowly and calmly towards her, but his legs carried him quickly. Out of the corner of his eye, he could see the little yellow bird flying from one tree to another.

"Eva," he said softly.

Eva turned and looked at him. She was angry.

"What?" answered Eva. Her voice was cold.

"You have to believe me, Eva. Something strange is happening. When I was at the computer just now, the words 'Take it back' appeared."

"Take what back?" asked Eva. "What are you talking about?"

It's time to show her the pendant, thought Lucho. His grandmother had told him that one day the pendant would ask him to take it back home. Eva could help him. He put his hand in his pocket and brought out the blue bag.

"Look," he said. "I have never shown this to anybody."

"What is it?" asked Eva.

"It's a pendant. I think it might be *guaca*," he answered.

Lucho gave the blue bag to Eva. She opened it carefully and took out the pendant.

"Isn't it beautiful?" asked Lucho.

"It's very beautiful," Eva said quietly.

"My grandmother gave it to me," he explained. "She said I had to take care of it, but that one day it would ask me to take it home. I used it to draw the mind map yesterday. I couldn't think what to write in the circles, so I stopped. When I opened my notebook in the library, I saw those words for the first time. I'm telling the truth. I promise, Eva."

Eva put the pendant back into the blue bag and gave it back to Lucho.

"My grandmother's name was Esmeralda," continued Lucho. "When she was working at the hotel, an American man gave her the pendant to take care of while he went to Bogotá. The man never returned. I don't know the name of the hotel, but maybe it was the Hotel Continental. I tried to find some information about it on the Internet, but I couldn't."

Eva's phone beeped loudly and they both jumped. She had received a message.

"What's wrong?" asked Lucho.

"The message," she said slowly. "It says 'Take it back.'"

"The same message as the one on the computer screen!" said Lucho slowly. "Eva, I'm not sure, but I think the pendant is asking us to help it. I think it's asking us to take it home."

"But that's impossible," said Eva. "That would be magic."

Lucho didn't know what to say. So many strange things had happened since he had seen the little yellow bird outside the history class window. And now the same message had appeared on the computer screen and on Eva's phone. Eva was right. It *was* like magic.

"Eva," he said, "will you help me?"

3 Read the extract again. Mark the sentences T (true) or F (false).

1 This is the first time that Lucho has seen the yellow bird.
2 Eva is upset with Lucho.
3 Lucho's grandmother bought the pendant.
4 Lucho tried to research the Hotel Continental on the Internet.
5 Lucho thinks the pendant is trying to send them a message.
6 The children can't understand the message on Eva's phone.

SPEAKING

Answer the questions in pairs.

1 What do you think is the story behind the pendant?
2 What do you think happens next in the story?
3 What other stories can you think of that involve magical or mysterious objects?

FUNCTIONS
Talking about sequence

Work in pairs. In what order do these things happen when an airplane takes off? Discuss your ideas.

First, I think ...   After that, ...
Next, ...   Finally, ...

The engine is powered up.

The wheels are pulled up.

The nose is lifted into the air.

The brakes are taken off.

The plane is turned in the air.

The plane is lined up on the runway.

WRITING
Explaining how things are done

1 Read the explanation and check your answers to the last exercise.

How do planes take off?

To get an airplane into the air, you need the correct airspeed. Airspeed is not the speed of the plane, but how fast the air is moving over it. If the plane is facing a strong wind, the airspeed is already very high. That's why planes are usually lined up to take off facing into the wind.

The engines are turned up to a certain power. Then the brakes are taken off and the plane speeds down the runway. As it does this, air passes over the wings. The wings are curved on the top, so the air has farther to travel over the wings than under the wings, and has to travel faster. This creates a force that pushes upward. When that force is great enough, the nose of the plane is pushed into the air. When the correct airspeed is reached, the whole plane takes off.

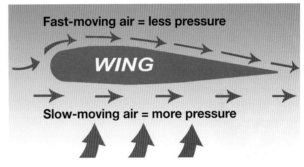

When the plane is high enough in the air, the wheels are pulled up and the plane is turned, leaving space for the next one to take off.

2 Read the explanation again. Use two different-colored pens to <u>underline</u> ...

• the **procedure** (what happens and in what order).
• the **theories** (explanations of why things happen).

3 Choose an activity from the list or your own idea. Write an explanation of how to do it (150 words).

• how to ride a bicycle
• how to play your favorite computer game
• how to do a headstand

Think about:

• the procedure and the sequence.
• whether you need to explain any theories.
• how to explain any difficult vocabulary.

READING AND USE OF ENGLISH
Part 5: Multiple choice

Workbook page 53

You are going to read a text about urban legends. For questions 1–4, choose the answer (A, B, C, or D) that you think fits best according to the text.

People have been telling stories for as long as they have been walking the Earth. And from cave paintings to Shakespeare's Globe Theater to Hollywood blockbusters, the methods of telling them have become more and more sophisticated.

In the 1960s, a new storytelling art form emerged – the "urban legend." Even if you've never heard the term, you've certainly heard an urban legend. What about the story of the unwanted pet alligators that were flushed down the toilet and are now living in the sewers of New York City? Or the man who woke up in a bathtub full of ice and saw a note informing him that one of his kidneys had been stolen?

One of the key features of the urban legend is its lack of an author. The stories appear mysteriously and are then passed on by word of mouth. Although we know these mini-tales of horror, humor, and embarrassment are almost certainly not true, part of us wants to believe them.

Then the Internet, which is packed with fiction (everything from jokes to the latest releases from top-selling authors), helped create and spread urban legends. Before the Internet, urban legends spread very slowly. They took time to reach a larger audience. The Internet changed all that almost overnight.

The Internet is the perfect vehicle for the urban legend, since it not only allows the stories to spread much faster, but it allows for greater anonymity, too – a lot of what we read online doesn't have an author's name attached to it. This anonymity adds to the overall mystery.

Of course, the Internet also allows you to check the truth of a story more easily. Over time, a number of sites have appeared that collect stories, investigate their origins, and report the results. Often there isn't any truth to the story at all. But sometimes an urban legend grows from something that did actually happen. Thanks to the Internet, learning about the origins of an urban legend can be as interesting and entertaining as the story itself.

1 What do we learn about stories from the first paragraph?
   A They've never been as popular as they are now.
   B They have their origins in the days of Shakespeare.
   C They were much longer in the past.
   D Ways of telling them have changed over time.

2 What does the author suggest about urban legends?
   A Everyone knows the term "urban legend."
   B Everyone knows an example of one.
   C They appeared at the same time as the Internet.
   D They're always about horrific events.

3 What does the author mean when he says that the Internet is "packed with fiction"?
   A You can find every story written online.
   B You can get most fiction for free online.
   C There are lots of stories on the Internet.
   D There are too many stories on the Internet.

4 What does the author suggest about urban legends in the last paragraph?
   A They're generally mystery stories.
   B They're usually short.
   C It's now easy to discover whether they're true.
   D Some include the author's name.

VOCABULARY

1 Complete the sentences with the words in the list. There are four extra words.

plot | setting | hero | character | opening | ending | villain | hilarious
miserable | terrified | fascinating | delighted | terrible | freezing

1 The special effects in the movie were great, but the _____ was boring.
2 The show that we saw in the theater last night was _____. I couldn't stop laughing.
3 The book was really good up to the last chapter. I didn't like the _____ at all.
4 My brother can't swim. He's frightened of water, and he's _____ of drowning.
5 He dived into the _____ water.
6 There is one _____ in the movie who is really funny. He makes everybody laugh.
7 I haven't done my homework. I had a _____ headache last night.
8 The story was so sad that I felt _____ when I had finished reading it.
9 I'm _____ that you can come and see the show. The other actors will be happy, too.
10 The _____ of the story is an evil vampire.

/10

GRAMMAR

2 Complete the sentences with the words and phrases in the list. There are two extras.

are used | have it cut | have been taken | whose | where | who | that | are pulled

1 It's a story _____ has been passed down from generation to generation.
2 Hundreds of photos of the magician _____ .
3 She's an actress _____ has a great talent for storytelling.
4 Jack grew his hair long, and now he wants to _____ .
5 Two rabbits _____ out of a hat in this trick.
6 He still lives in the city _____ he was born.

3 Find and correct the mistake in each sentence.

1 The decision will be done by the judges tonight.   _____
2 I didn't make very well on the test.   _____
3 The marathon will have shown live on TV.   _____
4 I won a medal for swimming, what made me feel proud.   _____
5 I'm not allowed have my hair dyed.   _____
6 Mrs. Jones, who son is in my class, is my piano teacher.   _____

/12

FUNCTIONAL LANGUAGE

4 Circle the correct words.

1 A You'll never *know / believe* what happened just now.
   B *What / Really*?
   A I guessed all the answers in the TV game show correctly. What are the *chances / possibilities* of that?
2 A What's that song you keep singing?
   B That's the *annoying / angry* thing! I can't remember what it's called or who sings it.
3 A How does this machine work?
   B First, the engine *is / was* turned on. After *it / that*, the handbrake is released.
4 A I *had / made* my nose pierced yesterday. Do you like it?
   B No, I don't. And your dad's going to *kill / hurt* you when he sees it.

/8

MY SCORE   /30

| 22 – 30 |
| 10 – 21 |
| 0 – 9 |

PRONUNCIATION

UNIT 1
Linking words with *up*

1 🔊 1.11 **Read and listen to the dialogue.**

STEVE   What's **up**, Jenny?

JENNY   I'm tired! **I'm up** late every night studying.

STEVE   You need your sleep! Can't you ge**t up** later?

JENNY   Not really. I've take**n up** the flute this year, and I practice in the mornings.

STEVE   Well, it'**s up** to you, but I'd quit!

JENNY   Yeah. I wish I hadn't signe**d up** for the school orchestra now!

2 **What happens to the words in blue? Circle the correct word to complete the rule:**

A word ending in a [1]*consonant / vowel* sound links with the following word when it begins with a [2]*consonant / vowel* sound.

3 🔊 1.12 **Listen, repeat, and practice.**

UNIT 2
Initial consonant clusters with /s/

1 🔊 1.14 **Read and listen to the tongue twisters.**

Strong winds **spread** the **sparks** through the **streets**.
Stella has **straight** hair and **stripes** on her **skirt**.
Stewart **sprayed** his phone with a **special screen** cleaner.

2 **Say the words in blue.**

3 🔊 1.15 **Listen, repeat, and practice.**

UNIT 3
Strong and weak forms: /ɑv/ and /əv/

1 🔊 1.21 **Read and listen to the dialogue.**

JULIA   What do you always buy the same brand **of**?

JACK   I always buy the same brand **of** sneakers. They're called Ace. I bought a pair **of** green ones last week.

JULIA   Ace? What are they made **of**?

JACK   They're made **of** fabric and rubber. They put a lot **of** effort into the design and quality **of** them.

JULIA   And into the marketing **of** them, too!

2 🔊 1.21 **Listen again and underline each *of* that is stressed and circle each *of* that is unstressed.**

3 🔊 1.22 **Listen, repeat, and practice.**

UNIT 4
Consonant–vowel word linking

1 🔊 1.28 **Read and listen to the dialogue.**

LISA   I was only joking, but I wish I hadn't said it. I think she hates me.

HENRY   Well, it was unkind of you to say you didn't like her new haircut.

LISA   I know! I can't believe I said that she looked like a boy! It just came out. What should I do?

HENRY   First, I'd apologize. Then I'd admit that I prefer it long. Actually, I think she looks amazing!

2 🔊 1.28 **Underline examples of linking in the dialogue. Then listen and check.**

3 🔊 1.29 **Listen, repeat, and practice.**

UNIT 5
/ə/ in word endings

1 🔊 1.36 **Read and listen to the tongue twisters.**

Ireland's a nation with famous traditions.
The warden's an excellent musician.
The goblin's a villain who frightens the children.

2 🔊 1.36 **Listen again and focus on the endings in blue. Are they stressed or unstressed? They all have the same short vowel sound. What is it?**

3 🔊 1.37 **Listen, repeat, and practice.**

UNIT 6
The /ʒ/ phoneme

1 🔊 1.39 **Read and listen to the interview.**

HELEN   Welcome to *Movie Night Television*. Our guest is Tom Potts, who stars in an unusual thriller called *Asian Treasure*. Why did you decide to take on this role?

TOM   It was a difficult decision, Helen. I play the part of an amazing illusionist.

HELEN   There are so many collisions and explosions in the movie that I thought you would never find that treasure.

TOM   It's true! Occasionally I was frightened for my own life!

HELEN   And the conclusion is certainly surprising.

2 **How is each *s* (in blue) pronounced?**

3 🔊 1.40 **Listen, repeat, and practice.**

This page is intentionally left blank.

GET IT RIGHT!

UNIT 1
Simple present vs. present continuous

It's common to confuse the simple present and present continuous.

We use the simple present to describe facts, routine activities, and opinions.

✓ I *usually go* there on foot.
✗ I *~~'m usually going~~* there on foot.

We use the present continuous to describe events that are happening now or around now.

✓ I*'m sending* you a photo of my new bike.
✗ I *~~send~~* you a photo of my new bike.

Find the error in each of these sentences. Rewrite the sentences correctly.

0   I know how hard you try to get on the team.
I know how hard you are trying to get on the team.

1   I think I am the person you look for.
_____
_____

2   I'm playing tennis on Tuesdays.
_____
_____

3   At the moment I write a letter to a friend.
_____
_____

4   I like what you wear today.
_____
_____

5   I know what you mean and are appreciating your help.
_____
_____

6   We are playing soccer for most of our vacation.
_____
_____

UNIT 2
Present perfect vs. simple past

Students often confuse the present perfect and simple past tenses.

We use the simple past when we include a past time expression to say when in the past an event took place.

✓ Yesterday I *ate* rice.
✗ Yesterday I *~~have eaten~~* rice.

We use the present perfect to talk about past events when we don't say exactly when they took place and with expressions such as *yet*, *before*, *ever*, and *never*.

✓ I*'ve* never *been* to Chicago before.
✗ I *~~didn't go~~* to Chicago before.

Make sentences using the prompts below.

0   we / see / the advertisement at the bus stop / yesterday
We saw the advertisement at the bus stop yesterday.

1   I / not see / the new Hobbit movie / yet
_____
_____

2   you / ever / go / to Chile?
_____
_____

3   John / take / his test / last week
_____
_____

4   Nina / get / here / a few minutes ago
_____
_____

5   they / not eat / at this restaurant / before
_____
_____

6   I / not eat / breakfast / so I'm really hungry and it's two hours till lunchtime!
_____
_____

Past continuous vs. simple past

> **Learners sometimes confuse the past continuous with the simple past.**
>
> ✓ *I was happy when I **came** in first in the race.*
> ✗ *I was happy when I ~~was coming~~ in first in the race.*

Which of these sentences are correct and which are incorrect? Rewrite the incorrect ones.

0 Last time I was visiting the library, I couldn't find the book I was looking for.
  Last time I visited the library, I couldn't find the book I was looking for.

1 When she arrived, I cooked dinner so I was a little distracted.

2 After that, I watched TV for about an hour.

3 As usual, we were arriving at about 6 p.m., then we had dinner.

4 My teacher came to see how our project went.

5 I'll never forget the time I was spending in Nepal.

6 The police saw the men and asked them what they did there.

UNIT 3
have to vs. *had to*

> **Learners sometimes confuse *have to* and *had to*.**
>
> **We use *have to* to talk about an obligation in the present and *had to* to talk about an obligation in the past.**
>
> ✓ *Shopping is stressful, especially if you **have to** find a particular item of clothing.*
> ✗ *Shopping is stressful, especially if you ~~had to~~ find a particular item of clothing.*

Which of these sentences are correct and which are incorrect? Rewrite the incorrect ones.

0 The trains were fully booked so we have to forget about that trip.
  The trains were sold out so we had to forget about that trip.

1 I'm sorry I can't go to class tomorrow because I had to go to the doctor.

2 My dad was going to work for another company, so we have to move.

3 If you want a drink after swimming, you have to go somewhere else.

4 If I have to choose between going to a small school or a large one, I would choose a large one.

5 Do we have to bring any money for the trip next week?

6 Yesterday we had to write an essay about Barack Obama.

don't have to vs. *must not*

> **Learners sometimes make errors with *don't have to* and *must not*.**
>
> **Although *have to* and *must* both mean something is necessary, *don't have to* means that something is <u>not necessary</u> whereas *must not* means that something is <u>prohibited</u>.**
>
> ✓ *I **don't have to** work tonight, as I've already finished everything.*
> ✗ *I ~~must not~~ work tonight, as I've already finished everything.*
> ✓ *I **must not** fail my test, or I'll have to retake it.*

Write the sentences with *must not* or *don't have to*.

0 You / stay out late or you'll be really tired tomorrow.
  You must not stay out late or you'll be really tired tomorrow.

1 You / finish your essay now. Mr. Hawkins said that we can hand it in next Friday.

2 You / bring anything to the party. Just bring yourself!

3 You / eat food in class. It's against the rules.

4 You / talk during the test.

5 You / review every unit. The exam only includes Units 1 to 3.

6 You / use your phone in class. It'll be confiscated.

UNIT 4
if vs. when

> **Learners often confuse *if* with *when*.**
>
> **We use *if* to indicate possible actions or events.**
> ✓ *It'll be best for us **if** everyone goes by bicycle. Parking spots are limited.*
> ✗ *It'll be best for us ~~when~~ everyone goes by bicycle. Parking spots are limited.*
>
> **We use *when* to indicate events that have happened in the past or are going to happen in the future.**
> ✓ *I can pass on your message. I'll tell him **when** I see him tomorrow.*
> ✗ *I can pass on your message. I'll tell him ~~if~~ I see him tomorrow.*

Complete these sentences with *if* or *when*.

0   I was very pleased _*when*_ I read your letter.
1   I had a great time _____ I went to Monterrey.
2   Would it be OK _____ I invited my friend?
3   I'll call you _____ I get home tonight.
4   Do you mind _____ we meet at 5:00 instead of 4:00?
5   _____ you're free on Saturday, come to the movies with us!
6   He went to Africa _____ he was 21 because of his job.
7   How much would it cost _____ we were a group of ten?

UNIT 5
Relative pronouns

> **Learners sometimes confuse *who* and *that*.**
>
> **We use *who* to refer to people and *that* to refer to things.**
> ✓ *Next week I'm going to visit my uncle **who** lives in Topeka.*
> ✗ *Next week I'm going to visit my uncle ~~that~~ lives in Topeka.*

Complete the sentences with *who* or *that*.

0   There are several problems _*that*_ can't wait any longer.
1   My friend Paul, _____ I've known since primary school, is coming.
2   Animals _____ can protect themselves shouldn't be kept in a zoo.
3   My dad works for a company _____ sells dental products.

4   It's a great movie, but it's really sad. It's about a soldier _____ dies in a war.
5   She was the only one _____ talked to me.
6   He's currently working for a charity _____ helps elderly people.

UNIT 6
absolutely vs. very

> **A common mistake is using intensifiers like *absolutely* and *very* with the wrong types of adjectives.**
>
> **We use *absolutely* to modify non-gradable adjectives or adjectives with a strong or extreme meaning.**
> ✓ *It's **absolutely** freezing outside.*
> ✗ *It's ~~very~~ freezing outside.*
>
> **We use *very* to modify gradable adjectives.**
> ✓ *I was **very** disappointed with it.*
> ✗ *I was ~~absolutely~~ disappointed with it.*

Complete the sentences with *absolutely* or *very*.

0   In my opinion, the countryside is _*very*_ relaxing.
1   This museum is _____ fascinating.
2   The view from the top was _____ amazing.
3   I thought the lecture was _____ interesting.
4   The test was _____ impossible. How did you get an "A" on it?
5   This food is _____ tasty.
6   She's a _____ good singer.

STUDENT A

UNIT 1, PAGE 19

Student A

You aren't very happy with your brother or sister.
He/She plays loud music that you don't like when
you're trying to work. He/She doesn't even keep the
door closed. What else upsets you about this? You
have decided to talk to him/her about it. Try and use
the expressions in Exercise 1.

Excuse me, [name], I need to talk to you ...

STUDENT B

UNIT 1, PAGE 19

Student B

You aren't very happy with your brother or sister. He/She keeps taking your clothes without asking you. He/She makes a real mess when he/she takes them from your closet. What else upsets you about this? You have decided to talk to him/her about it. Try and use the expressions in Exercise 1.

Excuse me, [name], I need to talk to you ...

Acknowledgements

The authors and publishers acknowledge the following sources of copyright material and are grateful for the permissions granted. While every effort has been made, it has not always been possible to identify the sources of all the material used, or to trace all copyright holders. If any omissions are brought to our notice, we will be happy to include the appropriate acknowledgements on reprinting and in the next update to the digital edition, as applicable.

The publishers are grateful to the following for permission to reproduce copyright photographs and material:

Key: L = Left, C = Center, R = Right, T = Top, B = Below, B/G = Background

p. 4: ©ARENA Creative/Shutterstock; p. 5 (B/G): ©Triff/Shutterstock; p. 5 (R): ©Robin Marchant/Getty Images; p. 6 (L): ©Jubilee Images/Alamy; p. 6 (C): ©Nickolay Khoroshkov/Shutterstock; p. 6 (R): ©Richard Coombs/Alamy; p. 7: ©dwphotos/Shutterstock; p. 8: ©Tetra Images/Alamy; p. 9: ©Stewart Cook/REX; p. 11 (T, C): ©cobalt88/Shutterstock; p. 11 (B): ©artjazz/Shutterstock; p. 12 (C): ©Jacek Chabraszewski/iStock/Getty Images Plus/Getty Images; p. 12 (TL): ©Olaf Speier/Shutterstock; p. 12 (R, BL): ©Sean Justice/The Image Bank/Getty Images; p. 13: ©Ben Welsh/Corbis; p. 15 (L): ©David Fisher/REX; p. 15 (C): ©UNITED ARTISTS/THE KOBAL COLLECTION; p. 15 (R): ©Lipnitzki/Roger Viollet/Getty Images; p. 16 (B/G): ©Ensuper/Shutterstock; p. 16 (R): ©Jim Craigmyle/Corbis; p. 20 (L): ©The Art Archive/Alamy; p. 20 (R): ©Monkey Business Images/Shutterstock; p. 21: ©GL Archive/Alamy; p. 22: ©eelnosiva/iStock/Getty Images Plus/Getty Images; p. 24 (TR): ©The Art Archive/Alamy; p. 24 (BL): ©Classic Image/Alamy; p. 24 (B/G): ©RoyStudio.eu/Shutterstock; p. 25 (TR): ©frescomovie/Shutterstock; p. 25 (L): ©Tomsickova Tatyana/Shutterstock; p. 25 (B): ©Dmitry Naumov/iStock/Getty Images Plus/Getty Images; p. 26 (TR): ©PavelSvoboda/Shutterstock; p. 26 (BL): ©Steven Kazlowski/Science Faction/Getty Images; p. 26 (B/G): ©Rigamondis/Shutterstock; p. 27: ©Agencja Fotograficzna Caro/Alamy; p. 28: ©Accord/Shutterstock; p. 30 (TL): ©Swatch; p. 30 (TR): ©WhatsApp; p. 30 (BL): ©Jaguar; p. 30 (BR): ©Pret A Manger; p. 30-31 (B/G): ©POMACHKA/iStock/Getty Images Plus/Getty Images; p. 32: ©Kevin Dodge/Corbis; p. 33: ©Beau Lark/Corbis; p. 34 (TL): ©Alberto E. Rodriguez/Getty Images; p. 34 (TR): ©REX; p. 34 (B): ©roundstripe/Shutterstock; p. 36 (TR): ©nito/Shutterstock; p. 36 (C): Complete front cover: Wild Country Level 3 Lower Intermediate (2008) by Margaret Johnson 978-0-521-71367-2. Reproduced with permission of Cambridge University Press; p. 36 (B/G): ©Anneka/Shutterstock; p. 37: ©wavebreakmedia/Shutterstock; p. 39 (B/G): ©happykanppy/Shutterstock; p. 39 (BR): ©shvili/iStock/Getty Images Plus/Getty Images; p. 40: ©Martin Novak/Shutterstock; p. 41 (L): ©Yunus Kaymaz/Anadolu Agency/Getty Images; p. 41 (C): ©WARNER BROS/THE KOBAL COLLECTION; p. 41 (R): ©AMBER ENTERTAINMENT/ECHO LAKE PRODUCTIONS/INDIANA PRODUCTION COMPANY/SWAROVASKI ENTERTAINMENT/THE KOBAL COLLECTION; p. 42-43 (B/G): ©Pawel Gaul/E+/Getty Images; p. 43: ©Feng Yu/Shutterstock; p. 48 (TL): ©Ethel Wolvovitz/Alamy; p. 48 (TC): The Hunger Games, copyright ©Suzanne Collins, 2008. Reproduced by permission of Scholastic Ltd. All rights reserved; p. 48 (TR): ©egal/iStock/Getty Images Plus/Getty Images; p. 48 (BR): ©COLUMBIA PICTURES/THE KOBAL COLLECTION; p. 49: ©jannoon028/Shutterstock; p. 50: ©KENZO TRIBOUILLARD/AFP/Getty Images; p. 51 (a): ©Julia Kopacheva/Shutterstock; p. 51 (b): ©S.Borisov/Shutterstock; p. 51 (c): ©Vitalina Rybakova/Shutterstock; p. 51 (d): Front cover of Darwin Edited by William Brown and Andrew c.Fabian - ISBN: 978-0-521-13195-7. Reproduced with permission of Cambridge University Press; p. 51 (e): ©andreiuc88/Shutterstock; p. 51 (f): Front cover of The Cambridge Edition Of The Works Of D.H.Lawrence, The Vicar's Garden and Other Stories Edited by N.H.Reeve - ISBN: 978-1-107-45751-5. Reproduced with permission of Cambridge University Press; p. 51 (g): Front cover of The University Murders, An Inspector Logan Story by Richard MacAndrew – ISBN: 978-0-521-53660-8. Reproduced with permission of Cambridge University Press; p. 51 (h): ©BrAt82/Shutterstock; p. 51 (i): ©Natalia Catalina/Shutterstock; p. 52 (L): ©WARNER BROS/THE KOBAL COLLECTION; p. 52 (TR): ©UNIVERSAL PICTURES/THE KOBAL COLLECTION; p. 52 (BR): ©PARAMOUNT PICTURES/THE KOBAL COLLECTION; p. 52 (B/G): ©happykanppy/Shutterstock; p. 53: ©WARNER BROS./THE KOBAL COLLECTION; p. 54 (T): ©David Soanes/Alamy; p. 54 (B): ©scenicireland.com/Christopher Hill Photographic/Alamy; p. 54 (B/G): ©Kues/Shutterstock; p. 56 (TL): ©Jason Kempin/FilmMagic/Getty Images; p. 56 (TR): ©Bobby Bank/WireImage/Getty Images; p. 56 (BC): ©Transcendental Graphics/Getty Images; p. 57: ©Jeff Moore/Empics Entertainment/Press Association Images; p. 58 (L): ©Ewing Galloway/Alamy; p.58 (R): ©kaisorn/Shutterstock; p. 59 (TL): ©Gari Wyn Williams/Alamy; p. 59 (C): ©Design Pics/Ron Nickel/Getty Images; p. 59 (R): ©Pavel L Photo and Video/Shutterstock; p. 59 (BL): ©M Itani/Alamy; p. 60 (a): ©Krasowit/Shutterstock; p. 60 (b): ©Evgeny Boxer/Shutterstock; p. 60 (c): ©Ian Walton/Getty Images; p. 60 (d): ©Chris Mole/Shutterstock; p. 60 (e): ©Josef Hanus/Shutterstock; p. 60 (f): ©vichie81/Shutterstock; p. 62 (B/G L): ©amgun/Shutterstock; p. 62 (B/G BR): ©Tarzhanova/Shutterstock; p. 64: ©Bartek Zyczynski/Shutterstock

Commissioned photography by: Jon Barlow p 18, 44.

Cover photographs by: (L): ©Andrea Haase/iStock/Getty Images Plus/Getty Images; (TR): ©Stephen Moore/Digital Vision Vectors/Getty Images; (BR): ©Pete Starman/Stone/Getty Images.

The publishers are grateful to the following illustrators: Bryan Beach (Advocate Art) 10, 31, 43; David Semple 17, 35, 55; Graham Kennedy 23, 63; Julian Mosedale 38, 59

The publishers are grateful to the following contributors: Blooberry: text design and layouts; Claire Parson: cover design; Hilary Fletcher: picture research; CityVox LLC: audio recordings; Silversun Media Group: video production; Karen Elliott: Pronunciation sections; Matt Norton: Get it right! sections

This page is intentionally left blank.

AMERICAN THiNK

WORKBOOK 3

B1+

Herbert Puchta, Jeff Stranks & Peter Lewis-Jones

CAMBRIDGE
UNIVERSITY PRESS

This page is intentionally left blank.

CONTENTS

Welcome 4

UNIT 1 Life plans	10
Grammar	10
Vocabulary	12
Reading	14
Writing	15
Listening	16
Exam practice: Toward First	17

UNIT 2 Hard times	18
Grammar	18
Vocabulary	20
Reading	22
Writing	23
Listening	24
Exam practice: Toward First	25
Consolidation 1 & 2	**26**

UNIT 3 What's in a name?	28
Grammar	28
Vocabulary	30
Reading	32
Writing	33
Listening	34
Exam practice: Toward First	35

UNIT 4 Dilemmas	36
Grammar	36
Vocabulary	38
Reading	40
Writing	41
Listening	42
Exam practice: Toward First	43
Consolidation 3 & 4	**44**

UNIT 5 What a story!	46
Grammar	46
Vocabulary	48
Reading	50
Writing	51
Listening	52
Exam practice: Toward First	53

UNIT 6 How do they do it?	54
Grammar	54
Vocabulary	56
Reading	58
Writing	59
Listening	60
Exam practice: Toward First	61
Consolidation 5 & 6	**62**

Pronunciation page 118   **Grammar reference** page 122   **Irregular verb list** page 128

A THAT'S ENTERTAINMENT!

Music

1 Unscramble the words and write them in the correct list. Add two more items to each list.

srumd | laslacsic | jzaz | oilniv
tagriu | opp | inapo | par

Musical instruments	Types of music
_____	_____
_____	_____
_____	_____
_____	_____
_____	_____

2 Complete the sentences so they are true for you.

1 I really like listening to _____

2 I never listen to _____

3 I play _____

4 I'd love to play _____

Verbs of perception

Complete with the simple present or present continuous form of the verbs.

1 Why _____ you _____ (smell) the milk?

2 What's for dinner? It _____ (smell) great.

3 What _____ you _____ (look) at?

4 You _____ (not look) so good. What's the matter?

5 This _____ (taste) awful. What is it?

6 Why _____ you _____ (taste) the soup again?

7 **A** Why _____ you _____ my coat (feel)?

  B I'm sorry. It's just so soft.

8 I like the way this sweater _____ (feel).

9 I love your new hairstyle. It _____ (look) fantastic!

10 Your hands _____ (feel) very cold. Are you OK?

11 She's _____ (not taste) the food for the wedding today. She'll do it tomorrow.

12 I don't like that new building. It really _____ (not look) good.

The big screen

Do the word puzzle and find the name of the biggest movie of 1997.

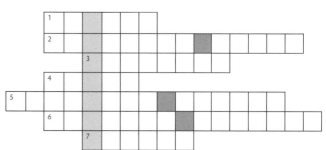

1 A movie that is full of explosions and car chases.

2 A cartoon style movie, usually for children.

3 An exciting movie full of suspense.

4 A movie with a powerful story.

5 A movie that makes you laugh and maybe cry.

6 A movie about other worlds.

7 A movie that makes you laugh.

Present perfect tenses

Circle the correct form of the verb.

1 I haven't *watched* / *been watching* TV for more than a week.

2 I've *seen* / *been seeing* this movie before.

3 The theater has *shown* / *been showing* the same movie for weeks now.

4 If you've *lost* / *been losing* your ticket, you can't come in.

5 They've *waited* / *been waiting* in line for three hours.

6 You've *read* / *been reading* the TV guide for an hour. Can I take a look now?

TV shows

Match the parts to make types of TV shows.

0	talk	com
1	game	program
2	drama	show
3	sit	news
4	sports	show
5	the	series

SUMMING UP

Complete the conversation with the words in the list. There are three you won't use.

're watching | 've been watching | the news
jazz | watch | to watch | watched
've watched | guitar | drama series

DANNY Ben, it's my turn ¹_____ something I like.

BEN Just give me 20 more minutes.

DANNY But you ²_____ your shows for more than two hours now. I want to watch ³_____, and it starts in five minutes.

BEN You can ⁴_____ it later. I really need to see the end of this.

DANNY What is it that you ⁵_____ anyway?

BEN *CrimeWave*.

DANNY What, that police ⁶_____?

BEN Yes. It's the last episode of the whole series. I can't miss it. I ⁷_____ all the others. I want to know how it ends.

DANNY I'll tell you how it ends. The policeman's the murderer. Now let me watch my show!

B TIME TO ACT
Our endangered planet

🔊02 **Complete the sentences with the words in the list. Then listen and check.**

smog | flooding | global warming
pollution | fumes | litter

1 With the Earth's temperature rising each year, many scientists now believe _____ is the biggest threat to our planet.

2 _____ from factories and cars are creating huge _____ problems, and many of the world's largest cities are permanently covered by thick _____.

3 There has been serious _____ across the area, and many people have had to leave their homes.

4 I get so angry when I see people throwing _____ on the street. Why can't they use the trash cans?

Question tags

1 **Match the sentences and the tags.**

1 You don't care about the environment, ☐

2 You want to help the environment, ☐

3 Global warming is getting serious, ☐

4 The world's not going to end tomorrow, ☐

5 You didn't go on the protest march, ☐

6 You threw your trash in the garbage can, ☐

7 The Earth can't take much more, ☐

8 Science can find a solution, ☐

a	isn't it?	e	didn't you?
b	did you?	f	do you?
c	can it?	g	is it?
d	can't it?	h	don't you?

2 **Complete the sentences with the correct question tags.**

1 You're from Argentina, _____?

2 This is pretty easy, _____?

3 You know him, _____?

4 They played really well, _____?

5 They don't speak English, _____?

6 She's working in Colombia now, _____?

7 He can't sing, _____?

8 He won't be late, _____?

9 You've been to Canada, _____?

10 I shouldn't say things like that, _____?

Indefinite pronouns

Complete the sentences with the words in the list.

everything | something | everyone | nowhere
somewhere | anyone | no one | nothing

The party was terrible.

1. I didn't know _____.
2. _____ I tried to speak to just ignored me.
3. There was _____ to eat at all.
4. You had to pay for a drink, and _____ on the menu was really expensive.
5. I wanted to leave my coat _____, but there was no closet.
6. It was so crowded there was _____ to sit.
7. I wanted _____ to do, so I walked onto the dance floor.
8. But _____ wanted to dance with me.

Party time

1 Match the sentence halves.

Am I ready for the party? Well, so far …

1. I haven't found anywhere ☐
2. I haven't gotten permission ☐
3. I haven't made ☐
4. So clearly I haven't sent out ☐
5. I haven't hired ☐
6. Or gotten the money to pay ☐
7. I haven't decorated ☐
8. And I haven't arranged ☐

a. a guest list.
b. the food.
c. a DJ.
d. a deposit for one.
e. the room.
f. from Mom and Dad.
g. to have a party.
h. any invitations.

Am I ready? Almost.

---

2 Complete the conversation with the words in the list. There are two you won't use.

something | everywhere | sent out
decorating | everyone | get | anyone
everything | hiring | nowhere
arranging | anything

MIA So, Jake, is [1]_____ ready for the party tomorrow?

JAKE I think so. I've just finished [2]_____ the room and [3]_____ the food.

MIA So, there will be [4]_____ to eat?

JAKE Yes, and to drink.

MIA So, who's coming? [5]_____ I know?

JAKE There'll be lots of people you know. I [6]_____ about 30 invitations.

MIA That's a lot of people. Did you have to [7]_____ permission from your parents?

JAKE Of course. I'm having the party at our house.

MIA Is there [8]_____ I can do?

JAKE Well, you could bring some music with you. I'm not [9]_____ a DJ.

MIA OK, I'll bring some music that will get [10]_____ dancing.

SUMMING UP

🔊03 **Put the dialogue in order. Listen and check.**

☐ a BOB Of course there is. I'm organizing a protest march for Sunday. Do you want to join me?

☐ b BOB That's too bad. But you could donate a little money, couldn't you?

☐ c BOB And I don't think the government will do anything about it.

☐ d BOB And that's why I think we should do something about it.

☐1☐ e BOB I think the pollution in our city is getting worse every year.

☐ f SUE I'm afraid I left my wallet at home. Sorry.

☐ g SUE So do I. It's a real problem, isn't it?

☐ h SUE Neither do I. They never do.

☐ i SUE But there's nothing we can do, is there?

☐ j SUE I'd love to, but I can't. I'm busy.

C IN MY OPINION, …
Feeling under the weather

1 Match the sentence halves.

1 Take this medicine, and you'll feel ☐
2 I always get ☐
3 Dad's going to the hospital to have ☐
4 Can you call the doctor and make ☐
5 Why don't you see ☐
6 You need to ☐

a sick when I travel by car.
b an appointment for me?
c a doctor about your headaches?
d exercise more to lose some weight.
e better in half an hour.
f an operation next week.

2 Complete the sentences with the phrases in the list.

get some exercise | feel sick | having an operation | make an appointment | get better | see a doctor

1 I hope you _____ soon.

2 Hello, I'd like to _____ with Dr. Hill.

3 He's _____ .

4 I think you need to _____ .

5 That dog needs to _____ .

6 I _____ !

Giving advice

1 Complete the advice with the missing words.

> I get really tired when I have to run.

1 You _____ exercise more.
2 You _____ to see a doctor.
3 You _____ to lose some weight.
4 You should _____ eat so much.
5 You _____ be careful.
6 You ought _____ join a gym.

2 Write one piece of advice for each of these people.

1 "I can't do my homework."

_____

2 "I'm bored."

_____

3 "I don't have any money."

_____

4 "I'm new at school and don't know anyone."

_____

Comparisons

1 **Use the words in parentheses and any other necessary words to complete the sentences.**

1 The Oscars are _____ (important) award ceremony in the movie industry.

2 The host wasn't _____ (funny) the guy who did it last year.

3 The ceremony was a lot _____ (long).

4 The best actor's speech was _____ (bad) I can remember.

5 However, I think the actors were dressed _____ (beautiful) than usual.

6 Apparently, one actress was wearing _____ (expensive) dress in the world.

2 **Complete the sentences so that they mean the same thing.**

1 It's hotter today than it was yesterday.
   Yesterday wasn't _____

2 I've never seen a more boring movie.
   That was _____

3 She's the kindest person I know.
   I don't anyone as _____

4 I used to remember things more easily.
   I don't _____

5 Martin and Steve play tennis equally as well.
   Steve plays tennis _____

6 It's the most expensive car in the world.
   There isn't a car as _____

SUMMING UP

◄))04 **Put the dialogue in order. Listen and check.**

☐ a BRIAN I'm going to. I made an appointment.

☐ b BRIAN I'm not sure. Every day I wake up more tired than the day before.

☐ c BRIAN I know. I'm not sure I can wait that long.

[1] d BRIAN I've been feeling really sick recently.

☐ e BRIAN The problem is it's for next Thursday. They didn't have an opening any earlier.

☐ f AVA Oh dear. What's wrong?

☐ g AVA You ought to call them and tell them it's an emergency.

☐ h AVA What? That's a week from now.

☐ i AVA Sick and tired. You should see a doctor.

☐ j AVA Well, I really hope he'll be able to help you get better.

D HELP!
Reported speech

Report the conversation.

0 JILL I need help.

1 SUE What's the matter?

2 JILL I can't find my key.

3 SUE Check inside your pocket.

4 JILL I've already done that.

5 SUE Have you checked the door?

6 JILL Why do you want me to do that?

7 SUE That's where you always leave them.

0 *Jill said that she needed help.*

1 Sue asked Jill _____

2 Jill said that _____

3 Sue told Jill _____

4 Jill said _____

5 Sue asked Jill _____

6 Jill asked Sue _____

7 Sue said _____

Sequencing words

1 **Rearrange the letters to make four sequencing words.**

1 rafte _____

2 hent _____

3 yanllif _____

4 ta rifts _____

2 **Use the words in Exercise 1 to complete the story.**

1 _____ we thought we'd never get out. The door just wouldn't open.

2 _____ five minutes of kicking the door, we were exhausted.

3 _____ Dad found the key in his pocket.

4 _____, we got the door open.

Asking for and offering help

1 Complete the words in the sentences.

1 Do you have a f_____ m_____, or are you busy?

2 C_____ I help you?

3 Can you l_____ me a h_____?

4 Could you h_____ me with something?

5 Do you n_____ any help?

2 Put the dialogue in order.

☐ a MIMI I said that I was going to clean it after I'd done my homework.

☐ b MIMI What deal?

☐ c MIMI Could you help me with my homework?

☐ d MIMI That's the same deal we had before!

☐ e MIMI But you said you'd help me.

[1] f MIMI Dad, do you have a few minutes?

☐ g DAD Clean your room, and then I'll give you a hand with your homework.

☐ h DAD And you said you'd clean your room – remember?

☐ i DAD That depends. What do you need?

☐ j DAD I'm sorry, but I'm a little busy.

☐ k DAD So I'll make you a deal.

IT vocabulary

Match the sentence halves.

1 Have you seen that Brian has posted ☐

2 Before you start you have to type ☐

3 I'm having a problem installing ☐

4 Send me the photo. You can attach ☐

5 I'm going to upload ☐

6 I'm sorry. I deleted your ☐

7 I'm not sure how to turn on ☐

8 It's taking a long time to download ☐

a all my vacation photos to my Facebook page.

b message. Can you send it again?

c airplane mode on this tablet.

d this program. Can you help?

e this file. It's really big.

f another message on the school website?

g it to an email.

h in your password.

Passive tenses

Rewrite the sentences using the passive.

1 Five people have posted new messages on my website.

Five new messages _____

2 Someone uploaded the video to YouTube.

The video _____

3 Someone had already typed in my password.

My password _____

4 Two million people have downloaded this video.

This video _____

5 No one activated airplane mode.

Airplane mode _____

6 The program is attaching the file to the message.

The file _____

SUMMING UP

Complete the dialogue with words in the list.

files | said I | buy | has accessed | said he
passwords | has been | delete | installed
is being | then

LIAM   My computer [1]_____ hacked.

KATE   What do you mean, "hacked"?

LIAM   Someone [2]_____ my computer from another computer.

KATE   Really? How do you know?

LIAM   A program has been [3]_____ that deleted lots of my [4]_____.

KATE   That's terrible.

LIAM   And all my [5]_____ have been stolen.

KATE   So, what are you going to do?

LIAM   My computer [6]_____ looked at by an expert right now. He [7]_____ thinks he can [8]_____ the program.

KATE   And if he can't?

LIAM   He [9]_____'d have to buy a new computer.

KATE   Well, if you do, remember to [10]_____ antivirus software.

LIAM   Yes, and [11]_____ create new passwords!

1 LIFE PLANS

GRAMMAR

Present tenses (review) SB page 14

1 ★☆☆ **What tense? Write SP (simple present), PC (present continuous), PP (present perfect), or PPC (present perfect continuous).**

0   I <u>haven't decided</u> what I want to do yet.   _PP_

1   I always <u>do</u> my homework when I get home from school.   _____

2   Liam <u>hasn't been doing</u> well at school for a few months.   _____

3   My sister<u>'s always talking</u> on her phone.   _____

4   They<u>'ve been thinking</u> about buying a new house for more than a year now.   _____

5   Jim<u>'s forgotten</u> to do his homework again.   _____

6   Steve <u>doesn't want</u> to go to college next year.   _____

7   It's the last week of classes, so we<u>'re not doing</u> very much at school.   _____

2 ★★☆ **Complete the sentences with the words in the list.**

've been writing | don't write | 've played
's playing | hasn't been playing | plays
haven't written | 'm writing

1   No, he isn't busy. He _____ cards on the computer.

2   I _____ invitations for my party right now. Can we talk later?

3   Most people _____ letters, just emails.

4   I _____ all morning. My hand's tired.

5   My cousin usually _____ tennis twice a week. He loves it.

6   I _____ to thank my aunt for my present yet. I must do that tonight.

7   We _____ all of these games. Do you have any others?

8   She's not very good at the piano. She _____ for very long.

3 ★★☆ Circle **the correct words.**

We ¹*take / 're taking* some really important tests over the next few weeks, so I ²*spend / 'm spending* most of my free time studying for them right now. Normally the two things I ³*like / 'm liking* most in life are TV and computer games, but I ⁴*don't watch / 'm not watching* any TV, and I ⁵*don't play / 'm not playing* computer games these days. I usually ⁶*help / am helping* my dad in the store on the weekends. He ⁷*doesn't pay / isn't paying* me a lot, but I ⁸*like / 'm liking* getting the money. I ⁹*don't work / 'm not working* there for a while. I ¹⁰*need / 'm needing* the time to study.

4 ★★☆ **Complete the conversations. Use the present perfect or present perfect continuous.**

1   A   You look tired, Paula.
    B   I am. I _____ very well lately. (not sleep)

2   A   _____ your homework? (finish)
    B   Almost.

3   A   Where's Bob?
    B   I don't know. I _____ him for a few hours. (not see)

4   A   You're dirty. What _____ ? (do)
    B   Helping Mom in the yard.

5 ★★★ **Complete the conversation with the verb in parentheses. Use simple present, present continuous, present perfect, or present perfect continuous.**

JULES   ⁰ _Have_ you _seen_ (see) Tara recently? I ¹_____ (not see) her for weeks.

DAN   No, but she ²_____ (text) me most days.

JULES   So, what ³_____ (do) these days?

DAN   Well, she ⁴_____ (train) really hard for the past month.

JULES   Training? For what?

DAN   She ⁵_____ (want) to be a professional basketball player. That new team, the Jupiters, ⁶_____ (invite) her to train with them. She starts on Monday.

Future tenses (review) `SB page 15`

6 ★★☆ **Look at Gillian's schedule and write sentences about her plans for next week. Use the present continuous.**

Monday	a.m.: fly to Madrid p.m.: have meeting with Paulo
Tuesday	a.m.: take train to Barcelona p.m.: watch soccer game at Camp Nou stadium
Wednesday	a.m.: fly back to New York

0 On Monday morning *she's flying to Madrid.*
1 On Monday afternoon _____
2 On Tuesday morning _____
3 On Tuesday afternoon _____
4 On Wednesday morning _____

7 ★★☆ **Complete the sentences. Use a verb from the list and the correct form of *going to*. Then match them to the pictures.**

see | not visit | study | move | not ski | make

0 We *'re going to see* a play tonight. I have the tickets.
1 The car broke down. We _____ Grandma today.
2 I _____ tacos tonight. I've just bought all the ingredients.
3 Sue _____ math at Boston University in September.
4 Paul hurt his leg. He _____ today.
5 They are selling their house. They _____ to Toronto.

 A 0
 B
 C
 D
 E
 F

8 ★★☆ **Read the sentences. Write *P* if it's a plan, *Pr* if it's a prediction, or *I* if it's an intention.**

0 I have a tennis lesson at ten o'clock. [P]
1 I called the dentist and made an appointment to see him this afternoon. [ ]
2 People living on the moon one day? Yes, definitely. [ ]
3 We decided where to stay in London – the Ritz Hotel. [ ]
4 I've decided what to do next year – travel around the world. [ ]
5 Will my dad let me go to the party? No way! [ ]

9 ★★★ **Rewrite the sentences in Exercise 8 using the correct future tense.**

0 *I'm playing tennis at ten o'clock.*
1 _____
2 _____
3 _____
4 _____
5 _____

10 ★★★ **What do you think your life will be like when you are 30?**

1 (be married) _____
2 (have children) _____
3 (live in a different country) _____

GET IT RIGHT! 👁

will vs. present continuous

Learners often use *will* + infinitive where the present continuous is needed.

✓ *I'm seeing the dentist because my tooth is hurting.*
✗ *I'll see the dentist because my tooth is hurting.*
✓ *I'm not sure we'll get it done in time.*
✗ *I'm not sure we're getting it done in time.*

Complete the sentences with a verb from the list in the correct form.

come | win | see | go | not go | have (x2)

0 I'm glad that you *are coming* to see me in Brazil!
1 We _____ a party next weekend. Do you want to come?
2 I think the Jets _____ tonight.
3 My brother _____ to college next week. He's packing at the moment.
4 I _____ to his party later because I have to study for tomorrow's test.
5 I know you _____ a great time in Rio.
6 Maybe I _____ you there.

VOCABULARY

Phrases with *up*

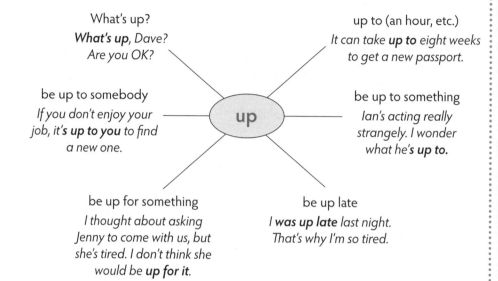

What's up?
What's up, Dave?
Are you OK?

up to (an hour, etc.)
*It can take **up to** eight weeks to get a new passport.*

be up to somebody
*If you don't enjoy your job, it's **up to you** to find a new one.*

up

be up to something
*Ian's acting really strangely. I wonder what he's **up to.***

be up for something
*I thought about asking Jenny to come with us, but she's tired. I don't think she would be **up for it**.*

be up late
*I was **up late** last night. That's why I'm so tired.*

Making changes

make a resolution
quit (something or doing something)
do well
struggle with (something)
take (something) up
break a bad habit
form a good habit
change your ways

Life plans

finish school
get a degree
travel the world
start a career
get promoted
settle down
start a family
retire

Key words in context

blame	Don't **blame** me for getting here late. I said we should take a taxi.
career advisor	The **career advisor** told me I should think about a job in politics.
criticize	Why do you always **criticize** everything I do? Don't I ever do anything right?
earn a living	He **earns a living** as a waiter, but he's really a musician.
good intentions	He had **good intentions** at the start of the year, but unfortunately, he forgot most of them.
intention	I'm sorry I said that. It was never my **intention** to upset you.
leave (something) to the last minute	Maybe if you didn't always **leave your homework to the last minute**, you'd get better grades on it.
lifestyle	He has a very interesting **lifestyle**. He lives half the year in France and the rest in the U.S.
plan	Who made all the **plans** for the party?
prediction	I'm not going to make a **prediction** about this World Cup because I think lots of teams could win it.
translator	My uncle is a **translator** at the United Nations. He speaks six languages.

Making changes SB page 14

1 ★☆☆ **Match the sentence halves.**

1 I've decided not to make ☐
2 I'm trying to quit ☐
3 He's on a diet and doing ☐
4 I'm trying to get in shape, but I'm struggling ☐
5 I need a new hobby so I've taken ☐
6 It's hard to break ☐
7 It's important for kids to form ☐
8 My dad needs to eat better, but he's never going to change ☐

a really well. He's lost 5 kilos already.
b with getting myself to the gym every day.
c good habits.
d his ways.
e up photography.
f eating chocolate, but it's so difficult.
g any resolutions this year.
h a habit sometimes.

2 ★★★ **Write down:**

1 a resolution you'd like to make for next year.

_____

2 something you'd like to quit doing.

_____

3 a school subject you do well in.

_____

4 a school subject you struggle with.

_____

5 a new hobby you'd like to take up.

_____

6 a bad habit you'd like to break.

_____

Life plans SB page 17

3 ★★☆ **Read the definitions and write the words and expressions.**

1 t_____ t_____ w_____: go out and see other countries
2 g_____ p_____: be given a better job (usually in the same company)
3 f_____ s_____: complete compulsory education
4 r_____: finish your professional life
5 g_____ a d_____: graduate from college
6 s_____ d_____: get married, buy a house, etc.
7 s_____ a f_____: have children
8 s_____ a c_____: begin your professional life

4 ★★☆ **Complete the sentences with the words and phrases from Exercise 3.**

1 My brother just loves being free. I can't see him ever wanting to _____ .
2 It's not easy to _____ a new _____ when you're 50.
3 Most people _____ by the time they are 18.
4 I certainly want to _____ one day. I'd like at least three children.
5 After college, I want to take a few years and _____ . I'd love to spend some time in Asia.
6 These days many people can't afford to _____ before they're 70.
7 I _____ from Miami University, but I've never really used it in my professional life.
8 If you work hard, you might _____ to junior manager next year.

WordWise SB page 19
Phrases with *up*

5 ★★☆ **Put the sentences in the correct order.**

☐ LINDA Why didn't you just go to bed?
☐ LINDA Really? What were you <u>up to</u>?
☐ LINDA Why? I don't understand.
1 LINDA <u>What's up</u>, Sam?
☐ SAM I was just playing video games with my dad. We were <u>up</u> until 1 a.m.
☐ SAM Well, we were playing on the TV in my bedroom!
☐ SAM Nothing. I'm just tired. I was <u>up late</u>.
☐ SAM I wanted to, but it wasn't <u>up to me</u>. I had to wait for my dad to finish.

6 ★★☆ **Match the underlined words in Exercise 5 with their meanings.**

1 doing _____
2 awake _____
3 didn't go to bed early _____
4 the matter _____
5 my decision / choice _____

Pronunciation
Linking words with *up*
Go to page 118. 🔊

READING

1 **REMEMBER AND CHECK** Answer the questions.
Then check your answers in the article on page 13 of the Student's Book.

1 What two resolutions has the writer recently made?

2 What has the writer done to try and lead a healthier life?

3 How is she finding it?

4 Why do scientists think we see our "future self" as being different from our "present self"?

5 How long does our brain need to get used to new habits?

2 Read the blog. How do SMART goals get their name?

SMART GOALS

It's that time of the year again that we all look forward to so much. Final exams! (I'm using sarcasm here, of course.) Well, this year I'm not afraid because this year I'm going to use SMART goals to make sure it all goes well. I read an article about SMART goals. They're what all successful people use, apparently.

So what are SMART goals exactly, and how are they going to change my life (hopefully)?

SMART goals are Specific, Measurable, Attainable, Relevant, and Timely. See how they get their names? No? Look at the first letter of each of the words. That's what you call an acronym.

Specific – because they are detailed. It's not good enough to simply say "I'm going to study for my finals." That plan's too general. A specific goal is something like, "I'm going to spend at least 20 hours studying for each subject and make a timetable to show exactly how I'm going to do this." That is a specific goal.

Measurable – because you should be able to measure your goals and ask yourself questions like How much have I done?, How much do I still have to do?, How much time do I still need?, Is this nightmare ever going to end? Well, maybe the last one isn't such a great example, but you get the idea.

Attainable – because your goal should be something that you can actually do. If your goal is, for example, to raise $1 million for charity, write a novel, climb Mount Everest, and study for finals, then you might want to ask yourself if you really can do all this and then maybe drop one or two of them.

Relevant – because all your little goals should help you work toward your big one. So, for example, a plan to help your mom and dad with all the cooking, cleaning, and housework might make you the most popular child in your house, but it isn't really going to help you with your studying, is it?

Timely – Your goal must have a time frame. In other words, it must have a start and a finish. There's not much point if you're planning to finish studying a couple of weeks after your final exams are over. That really doesn't make much sense. Likewise, you need to think about when would be a good time to start. And as they say, there's no time like the present.

I guess it might be a good idea to stop writing about SMART goals and start putting some into action. Goodbye.

3 Read the blog again. Mark the sentences T (true) or F (false).

1 The writer enjoys taking tests. ☐

2 The writer is going to use SMART goals to help her prepare for finals. ☐

3 SMART is an example of an acronym. ☐

4 SMART goals encourage people to do more than they can. ☐

5 You should plan a beginning and an end to your SMART goals. ☐

6 You don't need to think about when to start your SMART goals. ☐

4 Read the goal. Then follow the instructions.

My goal this year is to be healthier.

1 Make this goal more specific.

2 Write down what you can measure about this goal.

3 Write an example of an attainable plan and an unattainable plan for it.

4 Write an example of a relevant and an irrelevant plan for it.

5 Make a time frame for the plan.

5 Think of a goal you have and write a short paragraph about it. Is it a SMART goal?

DEVELOPING WRITING

An email about a problem

1 Read the email. Who is …

  1 Dave? _____

  2 Kevin? _____

  3 Conner? _____

  4 Gina? _____

2 Read the email again and answer the questions.

  1 What specific problems does Kevin have with Conner?

    _____

  2 <u>Underline</u> the expressions that show you he isn't happy with these things.

  3 What plans has he made to resolve the situation?

    _____

    _____

  4 (Circle) the language that introduces these plans.

3 What does Kevin do in each paragraph? Write a short description.

  A *He apologizes for not writing and offers some excuses.*

  B _____

    _____

  C _____

    _____

  D _____

Hi Dave,

A Sorry for not writing back sooner. I wanted to, but I've been pretty busy with schoolwork and soccer. Next week we're in the finals – very exciting. Here's a photo of us at soccer practice last week. We had just scored a goal! I hope you had a good time in Dubai – write and tell me what you did there.

B I've also been having a few problems at school recently with a new kid named Conner. The teacher asked me to help him out, and I was happy to do that. The problem is that now he's decided I'm his best friend. He's always sending me text messages and wanting to hang out with me. I like him, but if I'm being totally honest, I'm getting tired of him following me everywhere. He also gets really jealous and says some really mean things about my friends. Obviously, I'm not very happy about that!

C I know it isn't easy moving somewhere new. So I've decided that I'm going to do something to help him (and of course, help me, too). Next week I'm having a welcome party for him so he can get to know some other people and make more friends. And I know Gina wants to meet him, so I've given her his number. I've also told him about the youth club, and I think he's going to join it. The best part of that plan is that I can't go for the next few weeks because of soccer practice, so he'll have to hang out with other people.

D So that's my plan. If none of it works, I'm going to change my phone number! I'll write and let you know how it goes, but only if you write me back! Hope you're well.

From Kevin

4 Think of a person, real or imaginary, and write down three complaints about him/her. For each problem, think of a way of resolving it.

problem	resolution
1 He's/She's always …	
2 The problem is …	
3 If I'm being totally honest, …	

5 Write an email to a friend explaining your problems and what you're going to do about them. Write about 250 words.

CHECKLIST ✔

☐ Introduction

☐ Explanation of problems

☐ Say what you're going to do about them

☐ Say goodbye

☐ Informal email language

LISTENING

1 🔊 07 **Listen to Lucy and Carla's conversation and complete the sentences.**

1 Lucy is upset with _____ .

2 Will promised to help her _____ .

3 He arranged to meet her at _____ at her _____ .

4 Lucy wants to study _____ in college.

5 The application needs to be in _____ .

6 Lucy asks Carla _____ .

7 Carla says she's not good at _____ .

8 Carla is _____ in the afternoon.

2 🔊 07 **Listen again. Complete these parts of the conversation.**

1 **CARLA** What's up, Lucy?

   LUCY It's Will. _____ with him.

2 **LUCY** I can't believe he let me down.

   CARLA That's typical Will. _____ to do things and then forgetting.

3 **CARLA** Just text him and arrange another meeting.

   LUCY _____ the application needs to be in this afternoon.

4 **LUCY** Unless you could lend me a hand?

   CARLA I'd love to, but _____ very good at things like that.

DIALOGUE

Put the lines in order to make three short conversations. Write them in the correct places.

1 Making plans

A *Are you doing anything after school, Kim?*

B _____

A _____

B _____

2 Talking about intentions

A *When do you finish school, Ping?*

B _____

A _____

B _____

3 Making personal predictions

A *Do you think you'll have children one day?*

B _____

A _____

B _____

1 I'm going to study biology at Michigan University.

2 Two or three.

3 Probably. I hope so.

4 I'd love to, thanks.

5 Ian and I are going swimming. Do you want to come?

6 Next year in July.

7 How many do you think you'll have?

8 And what are you going to do next?

9 No, I don't have anything planned.

PHRASES FOR FLUENCY SB page 19

1 **Put the words in order to make phrases.**

0 silly / be / don't *Don't be silly.*

1 go / we / here _____

2 you're / best / the _____

3 hiding / have / been / where / you _____

_____ ?

4 start / where / I / do _____ ?

5 that / mention / you / now / it _____

_____

2 **Complete the conversations with the expressions in Exercise 1.**

0

A Should we invite Jim to the game with us?

B *Don't be silly.* He hates soccer.

1

A You look busy. Do you have a lot to do?

B Busy? _____ I have tests all week, I have to plan Sue's party, buy her a present …

2

A Can I make you something to eat?

B Thanks. I'm starving. _____ , Julia.

3

A I haven't seen you for weeks, Dave. _____

_____ ?

B Nowhere. I've just been really busy.

4

A I know you have to study for your final exams, but would you like to come for a quick bike ride?

B Well, I am busy, but _____ , I could really use a break. Let's go!

5

A Boys, get in here. You're ten minutes late!

B _____ We're in trouble now.

CAMBRIDGE ENGLISH: TOWARD First

Reading and Use of English part 1

1 For questions 1–2 read the text below and decide which answer (A, B, C, or D) best fits each space. There is an example at the beginning (0).

Teenage resolutions

According to a recent survey, more than 75 percent of 16-year-olds **(0)** _____ at least one resolution at the beginning of each New Year. The most popular ones are **(1)** _____ better at school and being nicer to family members. Other common resolutions include spending less time watching TV and **(2)** _____ playing computer games.

0	(A) make	B do	C form	D find
1	A studying	B making	C revising	D doing
2	A taking up	B struggling with	C breaking	D quitting

Exam guide: multiple-choice cloze

In a multiple-choice cloze, you read a short text in which eight words have been blanked out. For each, you have to choose one of four options to correctly complete the space. This question is designed to test your knowledge of vocabulary, including idiomatic language, phrasal verbs, and prepositions.

- First of all, read through the text without worrying too much about the missing words. It's always a good idea to get an understanding of the meaning of the text as a whole.

- Now focus on each blank in turn. Look carefully at the whole sentence that it is in and especially at the words that come before and after it. Maybe you can guess what the word is without even looking at the options. If you can, and your guess is one of the options, then this means you probably have the correct answer.

- If you can't guess the missing word, then look at the four options you are given. Place each one in the space and read the sentence to yourself. Which ones sound wrong? Cross these answers out and concentrate on the others. Make your final choice by going for the one that sounds best to you.

- Finally, if you really have no idea, then just choose one. Never leave an empty space on your answer sheet.

2 For questions 1–8 read the text below and decide which answer (A, B, C, or D) best fits each space. There is an example at the beginning (0).

Decisions

I'm just about to start my final year at school, and I still haven't **(0)** _____ what I want to do when I finish. I come from a family where everyone has gone to college, and I think that's probably what my parents expect me to do, too. But of course, it isn't **(1)** _____ to them. It's my decision, and the problem is I'm not at all sure what I would want to study there. When my parents went to college, it didn't cost much to get a **(2)** _____. Although both of them went **(3)** _____ to have successful careers, neither of them actually used the subject they studied. These days it's different. To go **(4)** _____ college is going to cost me at least $200,000, and that's only the **(5)** _____. I can't afford to study for a degree that I don't **(6)** _____ up using. I need to choose the right subject, and as I said before, at this time in my life, I have no idea what that might be. To be totally honest, I'd like to take a few years **(7)** _____ and maybe travel the world. Maybe with a little more life experience I'll be able to make a better decision before I **(8)** _____ down and start my career.

0	(A) decided	B thought	C settled	D fixed
1	A in	B for	C up	D out
2	A degree	B test	C form	D professor
3	A forward	B on	C by	D further
4	A to	B by	C from	D in
5	A price	B tuition	C fines	D bill
6	A start	B finish	C begin	D end
7	A over	B on	C off	D more
8	A live	B settle	C calm	D go

2 | HARD TIMES

GRAMMAR
Narrative tenses (review) `SB page 22`

1 ★☆☆ (Circle) the correct form of the verb.

1 He *was / had been* tired because he *ran / had run* all the way home.

2 My mom *was / was being* angry because I *was watching / had watched* TV all afternoon.

3 My friends *finished / had finished* breakfast before I *arrived / was arriving*.

4 We *had waited / were waiting* for the concert to start for an hour when they *made / were making* the announcement.

5 My sister *was studying / had studied* French for six years before she *went / was going* to France.

6 We *were / had been* at the beach for about an hour when it *started / had started* to rain.

2 ★★☆ Complete the sentences with the simple past or past continuous form of the verbs. Then match the sentences to the events.

0 Her car *was driving* (drive) through a tunnel in Paris when it *crashed* (crash).

1 The ship _____ (sail) across the Atlantic Ocean when it _____ (hit) an iceberg.

2 People _____ (dance) in the streets after they _____ (hear) he was finally free.

3 People all over the world _____ (watch) on TV when Neil Armstrong _____ (step) on the moon.

4 The crowds _____ (wave) at the president when they _____ (hear) the gunfire.

5 While people in the neighboring town of Pripyat _____ (sleep), a nuclear reactor _____ (explode).

6 While Amelia Earhart _____ (work) one day, Captain Railey _____ (ask) her to fly to the U.K. from the U.S.

Events that shook the world

☐ a Chernobyl disaster (1986)

☐ b Apollo 11 (1969)

☐ c John F. Kennedy assassination (1963)

[0] d Death of Diana, Princess of Wales (1997)

☐ e Freedom for Nelson Mandela (1990)

☐ f Sinking of the *Titanic* (1912)

☐ g First woman to fly across the Atlantic (1928)

3 ★★☆ Complete the sentences. Use the past perfect and the simple past once in each sentence.

Yesterday afternoon I had a guitar lesson.

0 When I *had finished* (finish) my guitar lesson, I *walked* (walk) home.

1 We _____ (have) dinner after I _____ (arrive) home.

2 I _____ (do) the dishes after we _____ (eat) dinner.

3 After I _____ (finish) the dishes, I _____ (call) my friend Tina.

4 I _____ (do) my homework after I _____ (speak) to Tina.

5 When I _____ (finish) my homework, I _____ (watch) a movie.

4 ★★★ What did you do yesterday? Write similar sentences as in Exercise 3 using the past perfect and the simple past.

1 Yesterday afternoon I _____

_____

2 After _____

_____

3 _____

_____

4 _____

_____

5 _____

_____

18

used to   SB page 25

5 ★☆☆ **Complete the sentences with verbs from the list.**

go (x2) | have | live | work (x2) | die | get up

In England in the nineteenth century …

1 Many children used to _____ in factories and mills.

2 They used to _____ very early in the morning.

3 They didn't use to _____ to school.

4 They used to _____ very long hours.

5 They didn't use to _____ good food to eat.

6 They didn't use to _____ on vacations.

7 They didn't use to _____ very long.

8 They used to _____ young.

6 ★★☆ **Complete the sentences about yourself with *used to* or *didn't use to*.**

When I was five, …

1 I _____ go to a different school.

2 My mom _____ wake me up at 7 a.m.

3 I _____ eat cereal for breakfast.

4 I _____ walk to school.

5 I _____ have a lot of homework.

6 My dad _____ read me a bedtime story every night.

7 ★★★ **Tony is asking Anna about her elementary school. Write the questions. Then match the questions to the answers.**

0 Which / school / go / to
   Which school did you use to go to?

1 wear / school uniform
   _____

2 have / a lot of homework
   _____

3 study / English
   _____

4 study / any other languages
   _____

5 What / favorite / subject
   _____

a It used to be math.   ☐

b Yes, I used to study French.   ☐

c Yes, I used to be really good at it.   ☐

d I used to go to Lincoln Elementary School.   ☐ *0*

e No, I used to wear my regular clothes.   ☐

f No, I didn't. Our teacher didn't use to give us much.   ☐

GET IT RIGHT! 👁

used to and *usually*

Learners sometimes confuse *used to* and *usually*. We use *used to* to refer to events that happened regularly in the past.

✓ *When I was in college, I **used to** work in a clothing store.*

We use *usually* to refer to events that happen regularly in the present. We do not use *used to* for this.

✓ *I **usually** go to the movies on Wednesdays because it's cheaper.*

✗ *I used to go to the movies on Wednesdays because it's cheaper.*

Complete the sentences with *used to* or *usually* and the verb in parentheses in the correct form: present tense or base form.

0 I   *used to live*   (live) in a really small town, and I really liked it.

1 We _____ (dance), (sing), and (put on) shows together when we were younger.

2 These days I _____ (go) to bed early.

3 They _____ (watch) TV on Wednesday evenings because that's when their favorite show is on.

4 Could you give us the 10 percent discount that we _____ (get) in the past?

5 He is more attractive than he _____ (be).

6 Do you _____ (wear) that funny hat?

7 She _____ (not work) late, but a big project is due tomorrow morning.

8 People _____ (not be) so busy in the old days.

9 That's the apartment where we _____ (live) before we bought our house.

10 People who _____ (get up) early often live longer.

VOCABULARY

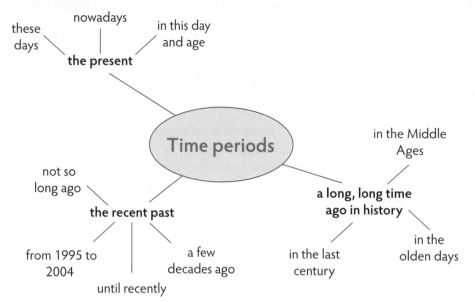

these days

nowadays

in this day and age

the present

Time periods

in the Middle Ages

a long, long time ago in history

not so long ago

the recent past

from 1995 to 2004

until recently

a few decades ago

in the last century

in the olden days

Descriptive verbs

dive

flee

rage

scream

demolish

smash

grab

Key words in context

accuse	They **accused** him of lying.
break out	The fire **broke out** just after midnight.
catastrophe	What happened is a **catastrophe** for the whole country.
disaster	The earthquake was one of the worst **disasters** that ever happened in that area.
elderly	Our neighbor is a kind, **elderly** woman.
fight (a/the) fire	It was difficult to **fight the fire**. It was so big.
flame	There was a big fire; people could see the **flames** for miles.
fuel	Wood, coal, and gas are different kinds of **fuel**.
household	These days, most **households** have two or three TVs.
lose (one's) life	More than 20 people **lost their lives**, and many were injured.
mattress	There were not enough beds in the house, so they slept on an old **mattress** on the floor.
oxygen	For a fire to start, three things are needed: a spark, fuel, and **oxygen**.
spark	A **spark** from a campfire can easily start a big fire.
spread	The wind was strong, so the flames **spread** quickly.
take (someone) to court	If you don't pay on time, they might **take you to court**.

Descriptive verbs `SB page 22`

1 ★☆☆ **Complete the sentences with the words from the list in the correct form.**

~~rage~~ | dive | scream | demolish
grab | flee | smash

0   The fire _____raged_____ for hours before they could get it under control.

1   The woman was leaning out of the window. She _____ for help.

2   The man _____ into the river to rescue the boy.

3   The building was unsafe after the fire, so its owners _____ it.

4   People _____ from the burning building.

5   The woman _____ her bag and some family photos before she ran out the door.

6   The man _____ the window to rescue the boy from the fire.

2 ★★☆ **Complete the crossword with synonyms of the underlined words in the sentences. Use descriptive verbs.**

1   Together we <u>ran out of</u> the burning building.

2   The girl <u>broke</u> the bedroom window.

3   "Help me," she <u>cried out</u>.

4   She <u>quickly took hold of</u> my hand.

5   Later, they decided to <u>take down</u> the building because it was unsafe.

6   They don't know why the fire <u>started</u>.

7   The fire was <u>burning very strongly</u> by the time the fire department arrived.

8   People were <u>throwing themselves</u> into the nearby river and swimming across it.

Pronunciation

Initial consonant clusters with /s/
Go to page 118. 🔊

---

3 ★☆☆ **Unscramble the words about fire.**

1   a m e f l   _____

2   a r k s p   _____

3   g e n y o x   _____

4   e u f l   _____

5   a s t e r d i s _____

6   a s c a p h t r o t e _____

4 ★★☆ **Complete the sentences about a fire with the correct form of the phrases in the list. Then number the sentences in the order the events happened.**

flames | spread | fight a fire | break out
catastrophe | lose (someone's) life

a ☐ The fire department worked hard, but sadly three people _____ in the fire.

b ☐ 1 It was late at night when the fire _____broke out_____.

c ☐ The firemen _____ bravely.

d ☐ The newspapers reported it as a

       _____.

e ☐ It was a windy night, so the flames _____ quickly before the fire department arrived.

f ☐ A man walking his dog saw the _____ and called for help.

Time periods `SB page 25`

5 ★★☆ **Match the two sentence halves.**

1   In this day and age ☐   a   not many people had color TV.

2   A few decades ago ☐   b   there were two world wars.

3   In the last century ☐   c   there was no electricity.

4   In the Middle Ages ☐   d   most people have a smartphone.

6 ★★★ **Write your own sentences using the time phrases.**

1   In this day and age _____

   _____

2   A few decades ago _____

   _____

3   In the last century _____

   _____

4   Nowadays _____

   _____

5   Not so long ago _____

   _____

6   In the Middle Ages _____

READING

1 **REMEMBER AND CHECK** Read the sentences and mark them T (True) or F (False). Then check your answers in the article on page 21 of the Student's Book.

1 The Great Fire of London started in a butcher shop. ☐

2 The wind was blowing from the west. ☐

3 The fire started in a wealthy area of the city. ☐

4 Some people escaped by jumping into the river. ☐

5 Luckily, the wind changed direction. ☐

6 A lot of people lost their lives, but not many buildings were destroyed. ☐

2 Look at the photo. Which century do you think the girl lived in? How old do you think she is?

3 Now read the autobiography and check your answers.

4 Scan the text and find three more words that show life was hard.

overcrowded _____ _____ _____

My name's Ellen, and I grew up in Manchester, England, in the 19th century during the Industrial Revolution. I was born in 1853, and at that time, Manchester had 108 cotton mills. It was called Cottonopolis.

Life wasn't easy for children in those days, and most children were dead by the age of five. Some might say they were the lucky ones because they didn't have to go to work in a mill.

By 1853 most people had moved from the countryside to the city for work, and the city was dirty and overcrowded. Three or four families often lived in the same house. We lived in one room in the basement of a house. It was damp, dark, and cold, and we only had one bed. The toilet was outside in the street, and we had to share it with all our neighbors. There

wasn't any running water in the house either. We didn't have any clean drinking water, and many people died from typhoid fever or cholera. My oldest brother died of typhoid two months before I was born. My family had only lived in the city for a year, and my mother wanted to move back to the countryside. My father decided they should stay in the city.

I was eight when I started to work at the cotton mill. The noise was terrible, and the air was filled with white dust from the cotton. I couldn't breathe, and I wanted to run away.

The mill was a dangerous place for children. I knew that. On my first day, a little boy died. He was sitting under the machines collecting all the waste when the accident happened. The managers were supposed to stop the machines for

cleaning, but they never did. Why should they? Boys like him had very little value.

One morning, after working there only a few months, I had a terrible accident, too. I was very tired that morning. I had already worked for three hours when, for just a second, I closed my eyes, and that's when it happened. A woman grabbed me and pulled me away from the machine, but it was too late. I had lost three fingers on my right hand. At the time I was happy about it. "Now I don't have to work anymore," I thought. But no, I was wrong. They found me another job – a job where I didn't need a hand.

5 Answer the questions.

1 Why was Manchester called Cottonopolis?

_____

2 How long had the family lived in Manchester when Ellen's brother died?

_____

3 Why did Ellen want to run away when she entered the mill?

_____

4 Where was the little boy working when he had the accident?

_____

5 How many hours had Ellen already worked when she had her accident?

_____

6 What happened to Ellen?

_____

GLOSSARY

Industrial Revolution   the period of time during which work began to be done more by machines in factories than by hand at home

mill   a factory where particular goods are produced

typhoid   an infectious disease spread by dirty water and food

6 Do some internet research about your country. Find the answers to these questions and write a short paragraph.

1 Did children under the age of ten use to work in the 19th century?

2 What kind of jobs did they use to do?

3 Do they still work in your country today?

4 What kind of jobs do they do now?

DEVELOPING WRITING

A newspaper article

1 Read the outline for writing a newspaper article. Match the information to the parts of the article.

introduction | main body | conclusion | lead sentence | headline

1 _____ This paragraph answers the questions "what?," "where?," "when?," and "how?"

2 _____ This paragraph (or paragraphs) gives more details and background information. Action verbs are used to make the article interesting and more dramatic.

3 _____ This is like a title for the article and tries to catch the reader's attention.

4 _____ This is usually a memorable sentence to end the article.

5 _____ This is usually a short opening sentence that summarizes the article and answers the question "who?"

2 Now read the article and label it 1–5 for the parts from Exercise 1.

AUGUST 31, 1997

☐ # Tragedy in Paris

☐ **Princess Diana has died after a car crash.**

☐ Tragedy struck late last night as Princess Diana left the Ritz Hotel with Dodi al-Fayed. They were traveling in a car across Paris when, at 35 minutes after midnight, the car crashed in the Alma tunnel below the River Seine.

☐ Photographers were chasing the car on motorcycles, and the driver of the car was driving very fast. They crashed into the wall of the tunnel. French radio reported that a spokesperson for the royal family expressed anger with press photographers who relentlessly followed Princess Diana.

Dodi al-Fayed and the driver died at the scene. The Princess and her bodyguard, Trevor Rees-Jones, were rushed to the hospital in an ambulance in the early hours of Sunday morning. Her bodyguard survived. Surgeons tried for two hours to save Diana's life, but she died at 3 a.m.

☐ This morning, the world woke up to the shocking news that Princess Diana was dead.

3 Now read the news story again and find the answers to the questions. Write sentences.

1 Who?

_____

2 What?

_____

3 Where?

_____

4 When?

_____

5 How?

_____

4 Write an article for the school newspaper about a dramatic event in your town. This can be true or something that you make up. Ask yourself the questions in Exercise 3 and use the answers to plan your article. Write about 200 words.

CHECKLIST ✔

☐ Use narrative tenses
☐ Follow the outline for an article
☐ Use action words
☐ Check spelling and punctuation

LISTENING

1 🔊09 Listen to a conversation about schools in Britain in the 19th century. Which subjects did children use to have to study? ⟨Circle⟩ A, B, or C.

A math, reading, and writing **B** math, chemistry, and physics **C** reading, writing, and geography

2 🔊09 Listen again and match the sentence halves.

1	Before 1870, only boys	a	playgrounds for boys and girls.
2	After 1870, all children	b	at 5 p.m.
3	They used to have separate	c	posters on the walls.
4	They didn't use to have any	d	used to go to school.
5	In the olden days, not many men	e	so they could walk home for lunch.
6	They didn't use to teach	f	used to become teachers.
7	They used to finish school	g	aged five to ten had to go to school.
8	They used to have a two-hour lunch break	h	geography in school.

DIALOGUE

1 Put the lines in order to make a conversation between father and son.

a ☐ **DAD** No, the Millennium Bridge didn't use to be here either.

b ☐ **DAD** Yes, it did. It used to be a power plant.

c [1] **DAD** I used to walk along here every afternoon after school.

d ☐ **DAD** It's completely changed. The Globe Theatre didn't use to be here.

e ☐ **DAD** That's the Tate Modern. It's a big modern art gallery.

f ☐ **SON** And what's that huge building over there?

g ☐ **SON** Did it always use to look like that?

h ☐ **SON** It didn't? What about this bridge?

i ☐ **SON** Lucky you, Dad! Has much changed?

2 Complete the dialogues with the phrases.

use to watch | your favorite meal
the other children | used to play soccer
in those days | school lunches

1

TINA What did you use to do after school?

DAD I used to meet up with
_____ in the
neighborhood. If it was raining,
we used to play board games
indoors. If the weather was nice, we
_____ in the park.

2

DEAN What kinds of shows did you
_____, Grandma?

GRANDMA I liked movies, especially musicals. They
weren't in color though. They were all in
black and white _____.

3

TONY Did you use to take your lunch to school,
Mom?

MOM No, I didn't. We used to get the
_____. The menu was the
same every week or every two weeks.
I can still remember every single meal.

TONY What was _____?

MOM I can tell you my least favorite meal –
beef, beets, and mashed potatoes.

Speaking part 1

Exam guide: Interview

In the First speaking exam, there will be two examiners and two candidates in the room. You will have a conversation with one of the examiners (the interlocutor). The other examiner (the assessor) will just listen. You will be examined on your ability to talk naturally to the examiner. Part 1 will last for 1½ minutes.

- First, the examiner will say:
  Good morning / afternoon / evening.
  My name is … and this is my colleague …
  And your names are?

- Then the examiner will ask you questions from certain categories, such as:
  1 People you know
  2 Things you like
  3 Places you go

1 Match the questions to the categories above. Write the number.

1 What's your favorite subject at school? Why do you like it? `2`
2 Who are you most like in your family? Tell me about him/her. ☐
3 Do you like reading? What do you like to read? Why? ☐
4 Are there any nice places to go in your town? What are they? What makes them nice? ☐
5 Do you have a best friend? Tell me about him/her. ☐
6 Do you enjoy using the Internet in your free time? Why / Why not? ☐
7 Tell us about a good teacher you've had. ☐
8 Tell us about the things you like doing on the weekend. ☐
9 Where would you like to go on your next vacation? Why would you like to go there? ☐

Exam guide: Interview

- As well as answering the questions, you need to give some details and opinions. For example:
  Do you like reading?
  Yes, I love reading. I just finished a great horror story called "Anya's Ghost."
- Keep your answers short, but try to make them interesting.
- Ask the examiner to repeat the question if you need him/her to.
- Don't forget to speak clearly.

2 🔊 10 Now listen to the interview with a candidate. How well did she do? Grade her performance. Give her 1 star for "could do better," 2 stars for "good," and 3 stars for "excellent."

		★	★★	★★★
1	She gives the correct responses.	★	★★	★★★
2	Her voice is clear.	★	★★	★★★
3	Her word and sentence stress are good.	★	★★	★★★
4	She talks fluently.	★	★★	★★★
5	She uses good vocabulary.	★	★★	★★★
6	She sounds natural.	★	★★	★★★

3 Imagine you are an exam candidate yourself. Answer the questions from Exercise 1 and ask a friend to listen to you and grade your performance.

CONSOLIDATION

LISTENING

1 🔊 **11** Listen and (circle) A, B, or C.

1 What does the girl not want to do when she graduates?
  A make plans
  B start working
  C go to college

2 The girl says she could work in a factory …
  A if the money is good.
  B for a short time.
  C for a long time.

3 Why does the girl not want to be like her father?
  A He works evenings and weekends.
  B He doesn't like his job.
  C He doesn't earn much money.

2 🔊 **11** Listen again and answer the questions.

1 Why doesn't the girl want to go to college?

_____

2 What does she say about the job market right now?

_____

3 What kind of job does she want?

_____

4 Why does she think working in a factory could be OK?

_____

5 What does she think is good about a 9-to-5 job?

_____

GRAMMAR

3 (Circle) the correct options.

1 I *go / 'm going* for a walk in the park every weekend.

2 Max and I *go / are going* for a walk tomorrow morning.

3 When I arrived, the place was empty. Everyone *went / had gone* home.

4 I used to *going / go* and play by the river every day.

5 In the future, life *is being / will be* very different from today.

6 The movie ended, so I *had gone / went* to bed.

7 Tomorrow I *'m meeting / meet* my friends in town.

8 Many years ago, my family *usually lived / used to live* in a very small apartment.

VOCABULARY

4 Complete the sentences with one word.

1 In this _____ and age, almost everyone knows how to use a computer.

2 I've _____ a resolution to never eat chocolate again.

3 She only started working here last month, but she's already gotten _____ .

4 I want to travel. I don't want to get married and settle _____ .

5 Is this song from the 1970s or the 1980s? Well, it's a song from a few _____ ago, anyway.

6 He went to college and got a _____ in math.

7 The firemen _____ the fire for hours before they managed to put it out.

8 As you get older, it becomes harder to _____ your ways.

9 The house was old and dangerous, so the city _____ it.

10 The post office said it could take _____ to two weeks to deliver the package.

5 Match the sentence halves.

1 When he reached the age of 63, ☐
2 The fire broke out because ☐
3 The flames spread very quickly ☐
4 When she stopped working, ☐
5 They were very scared, ☐
6 She decided to start a career ☐
7 It isn't a good idea to form ☐
8 My friend didn't do very ☐
9 It's up to you. ☐
10 I was up late. ☐

a to the next building.
b well on the test, unfortunately.
c in banking.
d That's why I'm tired.
e he decided to retire from his job.
f she took up photography.
g You decide.
h bad habits.
i someone carelessly dropped a cigarette.
j and they screamed very loudly.

DIALOGUE

6 Complete the conversation with the phrases in the list.

don't be silly | where should I start
now that you mention it | you're the best
stuff like that | here we go
where have you been hiding | what's up

JOHNNY Hi, Sophie! I haven't seen you in a while. ¹_____?

SOPHIE Yeah, I know. I'm sorry. I've just had so much to do lately.

JOHNNY Oh, ²_____ with the excuses. Like what?

SOPHIE ³_____? Studying for finals, taking care of my brother …

JOHNNY Your brother? ⁴_____ with him?

SOPHIE Didn't you hear? He had a pretty bad accident a few weeks ago. He was in the hospital for more than two weeks. He's home now. I have to take care of him in the afternoon when I get back from school.

JOHNNY Wow, Sophie. ⁵_____. How do you manage to go to school *and* take care of a sick person?

SOPHIE Oh, ⁶_____. There isn't much to it really. He can't get around very well, so I just have to get food and things, help him get dressed, ⁷_____. Anyway, he's my little brother, so I want to help him. I'm sure you'd help someone in your family, too, if they needed you.

JOHNNY Well, ⁸_____, I helped take care of my dad when he hurt himself a few years ago.

SOPHIE See? We all do things when we have to. And that's what I'm doing. It is tiring, though.

READING

7 Read the text and mark the sentences T (true) or F (false).

Charles Dickens and "Hard Times"

Charles Dickens was one of the most famous and successful writers in England during the 19th century. He became very wealthy and once traveled to the U.S. to give talks. His books are still popular today, and many have been made into movies – *Great Expectations*, *Oliver Twist*, and *A Christmas Carol* are some well-known examples.

But Dickens' life was not always an easy one, especially when he was a small boy. His parents had problems with money, so in 1824 they sent young Charles, who had just turned 12 years old, to work in a factory. He had to stick labels onto bottles full of "blacking," a polish for cleaning shoes. He was paid six shillings a week – that's about £12.50 a week in today's money. He hated the place.

A short time later his father was sent to prison because he owed money. This happened to many people at that time. Then the family house was sold, and Charles' mother, brothers, and sisters went to live in the prison, too. Charles never forgot this period of his life. As an adult, he wanted people to know about the terrible conditions that children often had to work in. And when he started writing, his stories were full of people who suffered the things that he had gone through himself. In fact, one of his novels is called *Hard Times*.

1 There are movie versions of some of Charles Dickens' novels. ☐
2 Charles' parents sent him to the factory because they needed money. ☐
3 Charles was almost 13 when he went to work in the factory. ☐
4 Charles' work was to polish shoes. ☐
5 Charles went to live in a prison with his family. ☐
6 In his later life, Charles wanted to help improve the situation for children. ☐

WRITING

8 Write a short paragraph (100–120 words). Imagine you are 12-year-old Charles Dickens, working in the factory. Say what your work is like and how you feel.

3 | WHAT'S IN A NAME?

GRAMMAR

(don't) have to / ought to / should(n't) / must SB page 32

1 ★☆☆ **Complete the sentences with the phrases in the list.**

go and see it | go to bed so late | buy a hairbrush | wear something warmer | be so shy | ask someone

1 You should _____

2 He shouldn't _____

3 I should _____

4 I shouldn't _____

5 We ought to _____

6 We have to _____

2 ★★☆ Ⓒircle the correct options.

1 It's a holiday tomorrow. We *have to / don't have to* go to school.

2 Well, it's your party. You *have to / don't have to* invite people you don't like.

3 Coffee isn't free here. You *have to / don't have to* pay for it.

4 Just your first name is OK. You *have to / don't have to* write your full name.

5 Well, those are the rules. You *have to / don't have to* be 16 to go inside.

3 ★★☆ Complete with *have to / has to / don't have to / doesn't have to.*

TOM Why do I ¹_____ go to bed now? Sally ²_____, and she's only two years older than me.

DAD True, but Sally ³_____ get up at 7:00 to go to school.

TOM Neither do I. It only takes me 15 minutes to get dressed.

DAD But you ⁴_____ take a shower, too, remember?

TOM OK, 20. But I ⁵_____ leave until 7:50. So I could get up at 7:30, so I ⁶_____ go to bed now.

DAD Well, if your mother says it's OK then we can try it. Remember, she's the one who ⁷_____ deal with you when you're tired and cranky in the morning!

4 ★★★ **Complete using a form of *have to* or *must* and a suitable verb.**

1 I'm going to a wedding tomorrow, so I _____ a suit and tie.

2 Josh, if you're going skateboarding, you _____ in the park and not go on the road.

3 He can't come out with us tonight. He _____ his brother.

4 In some countries you can eat with your hands. You _____ a knife and fork.

5 Her parents are rich, so she _____ about money.

6 Well, if you want better grades, you _____ more.

7 We _____ the dishes. We can put them all in the dishwasher.

8 My sister and I each have a computer now, so we _____ one anymore.

had better (not) SB page 33

5 ★☆☆ Match the sentence halves.

1 We must not be late, so ☐
2 This food might not be good anymore, so ☐
3 We've already spent a lot of money, so ☐
4 It's probably going to be cold, so ☐
5 My eyes are getting tired, so ☐
6 I didn't really understand that, so ☐
7 I think that milk is pretty old, so ☐
8 I hate it when you call me names, so ☐

a I'd better wear a sweater.
b we'd better leave now.
c I'd better read it again.
d we'd better not drink it.
e you'd better throw it away.
f you'd better not do it again!
g we'd better not buy anything else.
h I'd better not drive any farther tonight.

6 ★★☆ Use *'d better / 'd better not* and a verb from the list to complete each sentence.

apologize | call | eat | study
stay | invite | turn | wear

1 A We have a test tomorrow.
  B Well, you _____ tonight.
2 A My parents get worried if I get home late.
  B OK, we _____ too long at the party.
3 A I think he's pretty angry about what I said.
  B You _____, then.
4 A I have tickets for the concert tonight.
  B Well, you _____ Steve. That's his favorite band!
5 A I don't feel too well.
  B Well, you _____ any more potato chips.
6 A Look! That man's fallen down. I think he's sick.
  B We _____ an ambulance right away.
7 A The neighbors are complaining about the noise.
  B Oh, OK. We _____ the music down a little.
8 A It's a very special party tomorrow night.
  B Yes, I know. We _____ something nice.

can('t) / must (not) SB page 35

7 ★☆☆ Complete the meaning of each sign. Use *can / can't* or *must (not)* and a verb where necessary.

1 You _____ turn right.
2 You _____ park here.

3 You _____ go in here.
4 You _____ take photos here.

5 You _____ _____ here.
6 You _____ _____ here.

GET IT RIGHT! 👁
Confusion between *could* and *should*

Learners sometimes confuse *could* and *should*.

We use *should* to indicate that it's a good idea or that it's what will happen under normal circumstances. We use *could* to indicate that something may be true or possible.

✓ *If you want, you **could** bring some drinks.*
✗ *If you want, you ~~should~~ bring some drinks.*

Circle the correct modal verb.

0 Two hours (should) / could be enough to do everything. That's how long it normally takes.
1 I would like to ask if I *should / could* have another week to finish the project.
2 If you want to get healthier, you *should / could* eat balanced meals.
3 On the other hand, there *should / could* be risks with that plan.
4 *Should / Could* you please consider my application and look at my case?
5 I think that we *should / could* drive around the lake. That bridge looks dangerous.
6 Maria didn't know whether she *should / could* call the police. Maybe it was all just a joke.

VOCABULARY

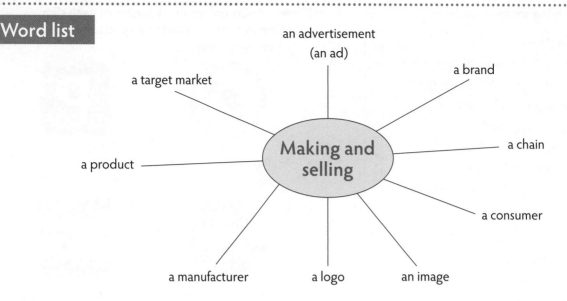

an advertisement
(an ad)

a target market

a brand

a chain

a product

Making and selling

a consumer

a manufacturer   a logo   an image

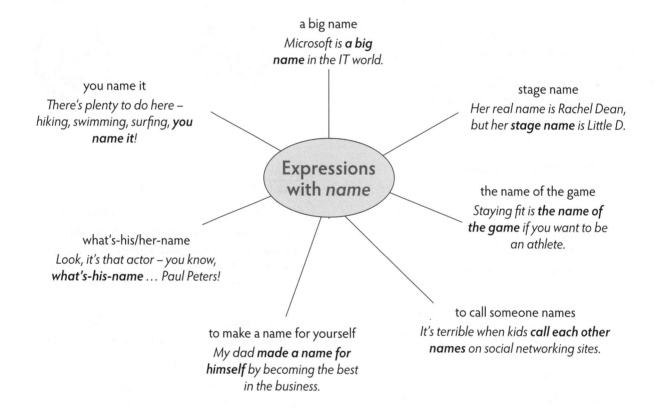

a big name
*Microsoft is **a big name** in the IT world.*

you name it
*There's plenty to do here – hiking, swimming, surfing, **you name it**!*

stage name
*Her real name is Rachel Dean, but her **stage name** is Little D.*

Expressions with *name*

the name of the game
*Staying fit is **the name of the game** if you want to be an athlete.*

what's-his/her-name
*Look, it's that actor – you know, **what's-his-name** … Paul Peters!*

to make a name for yourself
*My dad **made a name for himself** by becoming the best in the business.*

to call someone names
*It's terrible when kids **call each other names** on social networking sites.*

Key words in context

approved	The **approved** uniform at our school is gray pants and a dark blue shirt.
blend in	The color of the animal's skin helps it **blend in** with its surroundings.
distinguish	It's important to **distinguish** between work and play.
household name	Prince William is a **household name** in the U.K.
impact	Our new TV ads had a big **impact** on sales last year.
make a fool of (someone)	I said a really stupid thing. I think I **made a fool of myself**!
memorable	It was a **memorable** day. I don't think I'll ever forget it.
permission	My mom didn't give me **permission** to use her car.
unique	It's the only one in the world. It's completely **unique**.

Making and selling `SB page 32`

1 ★★☆ Complete the phrases with the words in the list.

product | image | logo | manufacturer | consumer
target market | brand | ad | chain

1 a _____ of fast-food restaurants
2 a _____ of things like cars or clothing
3 the _____ that a company makes
4 an _____ on a website or on TV
5 the _____ that a company tries to sell to
6 the _____ that people prefer to buy
7 the _____ that a company uses to identify itself
8 an _____ that a company shows the public
9 a _____ who buys goods or services

2 ★★☆ Circle the correct options.

1 This store is part of a *brand / chain*. There are more than 30 of them in this country.
2 I love that company's new *target markets / ads*. They're so funny!
3 Some of the best car *manufacturers / products* are Korean.
4 This is my favorite *product / brand* of coffee.
5 The marketing department designed a new *image / logo* to put on their products.
6 Our company is launching a new *target market / product* next week.
7 There's a huge *market / product* for self-help books these days.
8 Many companies support a charity. It improves their *logo / image*.

Expressions with *name* `SB page 35`

3 ★★☆ Complete with an appropriate expression.

1 I eat everything – _____, I'll eat it!
2 Nobody knew him ten years ago, but he soon _____ for himself as an actor.
3 You've probably never heard of Peter Gene Hernandez, but his _____ is Bruno Mars.
4 Go and talk to that boy – um, _____. You know, the new guy.
5 Our business needs to reach young people, so _____ is social media!
6 If you're angry with her, talk to her about it. Don't just yell and _____ her _____.
7 Everyone knows who she is. She's a _____ in this country!

4 ★★☆ Complete the crossword.

Across

1 "Monkey" is not an __ name in Denmark.
5 I won my first prize today, so it's a __ day for me!
6 The company puts its __, a big check mark, on all of its shoes.
7 Their advertising had a big __ on young people.
10 This isn't my usual __ of toothpaste.
11 All you do is buy things. You're such a __ !

Down

2 You need your parents' __ to go on the school trip.
3 The girl tried to __ in with her new friends by listening to the same music as them.
4 It's a very expensive car. The __ market is super rich people.
8 It's one of a __ of 120 stores all over the country.
9 The company is trying to improve its __.

5 ★★★ Answer the questions.

1 What was the most memorable day of your life?
_____
2 What is your favorite brand of clothes? Why?
_____
3 Think of an ad that made a big impact on you. What impact did it have?
_____
4 What do you have that is unique?
_____
5 Who is the biggest name in sports in your country?
_____

Pronunciation
Strong and weak forms:
/ɑv/ and /əv/
Go to page 118.

READING

1 REMEMBER AND CHECK Match the phrases from columns A, B, and C to make sentences. Then check your answers in the blog entry on page 31 of the Student's Book.

A	B	C
1 Companies really want to find	was given to a car	on an English expression.
2 A brand name should be	especially important	and easy to understand.
3 The name WhatsApp	a name for their product	of the whole product package.
4 The name Jaguar	but it's an important part	that they won't need to change later.
5 Brand names are	unique, easy to remember,	to create an image of beauty and power.
6 A brand name isn't everything,	is based	for the teenage market.

2 Read the blog quickly. Which of the three titles is the best one?

A People's names aren't easy to remember.

B Why do we sometimes forget people's names?

C Why can't I remember things?

| FORUMS | MEMBERS | BLOGS | GALLERY |

Hi, Paul here. OK, I'm sure this has happened to you, too, right? Last weekend ¹___, chatting with some friends, and my friend Hannah introduces me to this girl who seems nice and starts talking to me. And then some music comes on, and I think, "Wow, this is cool music," and I want to ask the girl to dance – and then I realize I have no idea what her name is. Hannah told me, but – it's gone. And I'm too embarrassed to ask her again. So I ²___ and go somewhere else. Ridiculous, right?

Anyway, this morning I Googled "remembering names," and there was an article that said that if you don't remember someone's name, ³___ you don't have a good memory – it's because you don't care. That if you're not motivated to remember, you won't. Well, I'm not so sure. I mean, the girl was nice, so I was motivated to remember her name, ⁴___. And here's another thing the article said: Some people ⁵___ in their own memories. They say, "I'm not good at learning names." It says people don't remember because they think they're not good at it.

I don't know. What do you guys out there think?

Greg178: No, I disagree. The reason you don't remember people's names is that you're immediately focused on what they're saying. You don't repeat their name over and over in your head – well, ⁶___. Unless, of course, you're more interested in their name than what they have to say.

VVXX: Sounds right to me. Sometimes I meet people, and I know I'll never see them again, so I don't even try to remember their name. But if I think a person looks cool or ⁷___, then I remember.

JaneGH: It's not that I don't care what a new person's name is, it's just that I'm busy learning other things about them. I'm so busy ⁸___ their face that I forget to listen for their name. But all I have to do then is ask them!

3 Read the blog again. Put the phrases (a–h) into the correct places (1–8).

a but I got distracted

b don't have much confidence

c make an excuse

d taking in

e it's not because

f I'm at this party

g not at a party, anyway

h might be important

4 Read the blog again. Mark the sentences T (true) or F (false).

1 Paul met a girl named Hannah at a party. ☐

2 Paul found an article about remembering names in a magazine. ☐

3 Paul isn't sure if what the article said is true. ☐

4 Greg178 thinks what someone is saying is more important than their name. ☐

5 VVXX always tries to remember a new person's name. ☐

6 JaneGH concentrates more on someone's face than on their name. ☐

DEVELOPING WRITING

An email about rules

1 Read the email. What does Burcu want to know about?

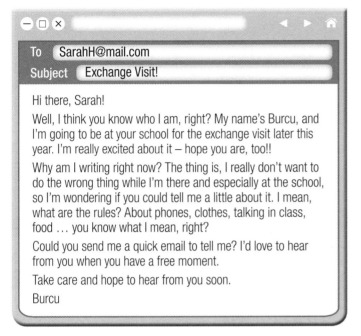

To   SarahH@mail.com

Subject   Exchange Visit!

Hi there, Sarah!

Well, I think you know who I am, right? My name's Burcu, and I'm going to be at your school for the exchange visit later this year. I'm really excited about it – hope you are, too!!

Why am I writing right now? The thing is, I really don't want to do the wrong thing while I'm there and especially at the school, so I'm wondering if you could tell me a little about it. I mean, what are the rules? About phones, clothes, talking in class, food … you know what I mean, right?

Could you send me a quick email to tell me? I'd love to hear from you when you have a free moment.

Take care and hope to hear from you soon.

Burcu

2 Now read Sarah's email in reply. Answer the questions that follow it.

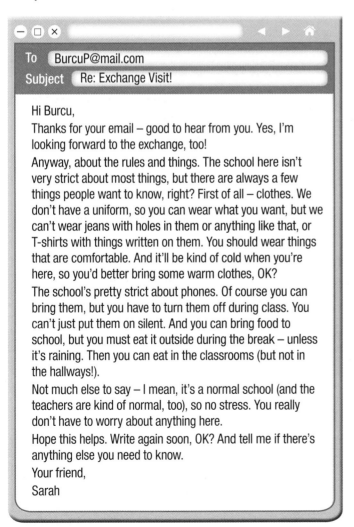

To   BurcuP@mail.com

Subject   Re: Exchange Visit!

Hi Burcu,

Thanks for your email – good to hear from you. Yes, I'm looking forward to the exchange, too!

Anyway, about the rules and things. The school here isn't very strict about most things, but there are always a few things people want to know, right? First of all – clothes. We don't have a uniform, so you can wear what you want, but we can't wear jeans with holes in them or anything like that, or T-shirts with things written on them. You should wear things that are comfortable. And it'll be kind of cold when you're here, so you'd better bring some warm clothes, OK?

The school's pretty strict about phones. Of course you can bring them, but you have to turn them off during class. You can't just put them on silent. And you can bring food to school, but you must eat it outside during the break – unless it's raining. Then you can eat in the classrooms (but not in the hallways!).

Not much else to say – I mean, it's a normal school (and the teachers are kind of normal, too), so no stress. You really don't have to worry about anything here.

Hope this helps. Write again soon, OK? And tell me if there's anything else you need to know.

Your friend,

Sarah

1 Which of the things Burcu asks about does Sarah not mention?

2 What are students not allowed to wear at Sarah's school?

3 What advice does Sarah give Burcu about clothes?

4 What do students have to do with their phones when they go into the classroom?

5 Where are students not allowed to eat at Sarah's school?

3 Answer the questions about Sarah's email. They are all about writing informally.

She writes, "you'd better bring some warm clothes, OK?"

1 She uses the word "OK" to *check for understanding / show disagreement*.

2 What is another word she uses to say OK?

She writes: "it'll be kind of cold when you're here."

3 "kind of" means *very / a little*.

4 Find and <u>underline</u> another time when she writes "kind of" in the email.

She writes: "good to hear from you."

5 She has left out the words *This is / It is*.

6 Find two other times when she leaves words out. What are these words?

4 Imagine that Burcu wrote her email to you. Write a reply to her.

a Think about the rules in your school and the things Burcu asks about:

- clothes
- food
- phones
- talking in class

b What other rules (if any) should she know about?

c This is an informal email (like Sarah's) – think about how you can make it easy for Burcu to read.

Write 200–250 words.

CHECKLIST ✔

- [ ] Include a greeting
- [ ] Use informal language
- [ ] Respond to all questions
- [ ] Sign off the email

LISTENING

1 🔊 **13** Listen to a conversation between Annie, Ben, and the new girl. (Circle) the correct answers.

1 The new girl's name is …
   A Maureen.   **B** Morgan.   **C** Morwenna.
2 She is from …
   A Cornwall.   **B** Wales.   **C** London.
3 She says that some places in Cornwall …
   A have nothing to do.
   B have names with strange pronunciations.
   C aren't very nice.

2 🔊 **13** Listen again and mark the statements T (true) or F (false).

1 Annie doesn't understand Morwenna's name. ☐
2 The name "Morwenna" is Scottish. ☐
3 A part of Morwenna's family lives in Cornwall. ☐
4 Morwenna says Newquay is a good place for surfing. ☐
5 The water in Newquay is warm. ☐
6 Ben pronounces Mousehole correctly. ☐
7 People in Cornwall don't mind if names are pronounced incorrectly. ☐
8 Annie gets Morwenna's name wrong. ☐

3 🔊 **13** Listen again. Complete these parts of the conversation.

1

ANNIE	I've never been there. To England, I mean.
MORWENNA	Oh, ¹_____ . It's really nice. And visit Cornwall when you're there. It's beautiful. My mum's got family down in Penzance, so we go there a lot.
BEN	Anything to do there?
MORWENNA	Sure. There are nice beaches, and if you like surfing, ²_____ Newquay.
ANNIE	But isn't the water really cold?
MORWENNA	Well, yes! So if you go surfing, ³_____ a wetsuit to stay warm in the water.

2

MORWENNA	If you go, ⁴_____ how to pronounce the names. Local people don't like it when tourists say the names wrong.
BEN	I think Annie's right. I ⁵_____ a new brain.
MORWENNA	What?
BEN	Oh, nothing. Listen, ⁶_____ back. Class starts in a few minutes.

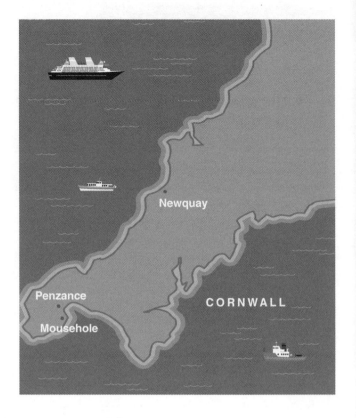

DIALOGUE

1 **Put the phrases in the correct places.**

'd better take | should know
should visit | 'd better learn

1
A You live in Vancouver, don't you? I've always wanted to go there.
B Yeah, that's right. And if you ever go there, you ¹_____ Stanley Park. It's beautiful!
A Is the weather nice there?
B Well, it can be OK in summer. But it rains a lot, so you ²_____ an umbrella!

2
A You live in Hamburg, right? I've always wanted to go there.
B Yes, I do. If you come to my city, you should see Miniature Wonderland. It's fantastic.
A Do you think I ³_____ German before I go?
B Well, you ⁴_____ a few words, I guess. But lots of people speak English, so you don't have to worry too much.

2 **Write a dialogue between you and a friend.**

The friend begins:

"You live in (name of your town / city), right? I've always wanted to go there."

Give the friend some advice about where to go, what to see, and what to do.

Use the dialogues in Exercise 1 to help you.

Listening part 1

1 🔊 **14** You will hear people talking in four different situations. For questions 1–4, choose the best answer (A, B, or C).

1 You hear a man in a store.
   What is the problem with the shoes?
   A His wife doesn't like them.
   B He doesn't think they're right for him.
   C They're too small for him.

2 You hear a girl talking about her hobby, sudoku puzzles.
   What does she say about them?
   A The puzzles are always easy to do.
   B She always solves the puzzles.
   C They develop her thinking abilities.

3 You hear a man talking about his trip to China.
   Which cities did he visit?
   A Beijing, Shanghai, and Chengdu
   B Beijing, Shanghai, and Xi'an
   C Beijing, Chengdu, and Xi'an

4 You hear a woman talking about getting to and from work.
   How does she travel?
   A by car
   B by plane
   C by bus

Exam guide: multiple choice

In part 1 of the First listening exam, you hear eight extracts – they are not connected to each other. You hear each extract twice.

For each extract there is a short statement saying what you're going to hear. Then there is one question. You have to choose the best answer from three options (A, B, or C).

- Read the questions and options in advance. It's important to get a clear idea of what you have to decide.
- The first time you hear the monologue, try to remove, if possible, at least one of the answers. Then, the second time you listen, you can concentrate on getting the correct answer.

- The speaker won't always give a direct answer. Instead, you will have to infer the answer – for example, we can infer "She is a writer" is the correct answer when we hear "She spends all day at her computer, typing out her ideas."
- Remember that you will hear things that are intended to distract you from the correct answer, so avoid making quick decisions.

2 🔊 **15** You will hear people talking in four different situations. For questions 1–4, choose the best answer (A, B, or C).

1 You hear a teenage schoolgirl.
   Why did she change schools?
   A Her old school was too far away.
   B She wanted to work harder.
   C The new school is cheaper.

2 You hear part of a radio interview with a man.
   What does he do?
   A He writes the words for songs.
   B He is a songwriter and singer.
   C He takes pieces of music and writes words for them.

3 You hear a woman talking about her hobby, birdwatching.
   How does she feel while she is birdwatching?
   A bored
   B hopeful
   C calm

4 You hear a boy who wants to be a chef.
   Why did he first become interested in cooking?
   A He ate some good Italian food.
   B He enjoyed cooking dinner for himself.
   C His mom cooked a fantastic dinner for his birthday.

GRAMMAR

First and second conditional (review)
`SB page 40`

1 ★☆☆ **Match the sentences with the pictures.**

 A
 B
 C
 D

1 If we lose this game, I won't be happy.
2 If we lost this game, I'd be very surprised.
3 If it snows tomorrow, we won't have to go to school.
4 If it snowed here, it would be very strange.

2 ★★☆ **Complete the sentences with the verbs to make first or second conditional sentences.**

0 I _will tell_ (tell) you my secret if you ___promise___ (promise) not to tell anyone.

1 Be careful. The cat _____ (bite) you if you _____ (touch) it.

2 If he _____ (be) taller, he _____ (be) a really good basketball player.

3 If I _____ (meet) the president, I _____ (ask) for his autograph.

4 Hurry up. If we _____ (not leave) now, we _____ (miss) the train.

5 If I _____ (know) the answer, I still _____ (not help) you.

6 If we _____ (not stop) talking now, the teacher _____ (get) angry with us.

7 I _____ (run) away if I _____ (see) a tiger in the jungle.

8 Our team is the best. I _____ (be) very surprised if we _____ (not win).

3 ★★☆ **Complete the sentences with the verbs to make second conditional sentences.**

What [1]_____ you _____ (do) if you found an envelope full of money on the street? [2]_____ you _____ (take) it to the police station? Or [3]_____ you _____ (keep) it and buy yourself something you really wanted? [4]_____ you _____ (buy) your mom and dad a present? If you [5]_____ (buy) them a present, they [6]_____ (want) to know where the money came from. If you [7]_____ (tell) them the truth, maybe they [8]_____ (not be) so happy. And if you [9]_____ (not tell) them the truth, you [10]_____ (feel) really bad. Maybe it's better not to find an envelope full of money on the street!

Time conjunctions `SB page 40`

4 ★☆☆ ⦶**Circle**⦶ **the correct words.**

1 Dad's going to get a new computer *when / unless* he has enough money.
2 I'll call you *until / as soon as* the plane lands.
3 We'll start the meeting *until / when* Mr. Benson arrives.
4 *If / Until* I don't pass my English test, I'll take it again.
5 You won't pass your driver's test *if / unless* you practice more.
6 We'll watch the game *as soon as / until* halftime.

5 ★★☆ **Complete the sentences with *if, unless, until,* or *as soon as.***

1 _____ we hurry up, we'll be late for the party.
2 Jim has the tickets, so we'll have to wait _____ he gets there before we can go in.
3 What will you do _____ we don't have any homework this weekend?
4 She can't talk because she's in the shower. She'll call you _____ she gets out.
5 I'm seeing John tonight, so I promise that I'll ask him _____ I see him.
6 _____ we can't get tickets, we can just watch the game on TV at my house.
7 I have to go to the store. Can you watch Tim _____ I get back?

wish and *if only* `SB page 41`

6 ★☆☆ (Circle) the correct word.

1 My dad wishes he *has / had* more time.

2 Paula wishes she *can / could* go to the game tonight.

3 If only the neighbor's dog *won't / wouldn't* bark all night!

4 The teacher wishes her students *weren't / aren't* so noisy.

5 If only I *am / was* taller.

6 Liam wishes Lucy *will / would* talk to him.

7 If only I *could / can* play the piano.

7 ★★☆ Read the sentences. What does Julia wish?

0 "My sister keeps taking my clothes."
   I wish my sister wouldn't keep taking my clothes.

1 "I don't understand math."
   If only _____

2 "The boys in my class are so childish."
   I wish _____

3 "I can't find my phone. Where is it?"
   I wish _____

4 "I can't afford to buy those new shoes."
   If only _____

5 "I want to stay in bed, but I have to go to school."
   I wish _____

6 "I have too much homework this weekend."
   If only _____

Third conditional `SB page 42`

8 ★☆☆ Match the sentence halves.

0 I wouldn't have gone to the concert   `e`

1 I would have gotten a much better grade   ☐

2 We would have saved a lot of money   ☐

3 She would have gotten completely lost   ☐

4 If you hadn't kicked the ball so hard,   ☐

5 If she had apologized,   ☐

6 If I had had his number,   ☐

7 If they'd been a little quieter,   ☐

a if I'd studied harder.

b if she hadn't had a map.

c it wouldn't have broken the window.

d I would have texted him.

e if I had known it was going to be so bad.

f they wouldn't have woken the baby.

g I would have forgiven her.

h if we'd eaten at home.

9 ★★☆ Read the story and complete the sentences with the verbs. Use either the affirmative or negative form. Then write two more sentences in your notebook.

My friend Dave threw a pencil, and it hit the teacher. The teacher was angry. Dave didn't say anything. The teacher thought it was me and gave me detention. I went to detention and met a girl named Sara. I asked her over to my place, and she said yes. Now Sara's my best friend.

0 If Dave *hadn't thrown* a pencil, it *wouldn't have hit* the teacher. (throw / hit)

1 If he _____ honest, he _____ to detention. (be / go)

2 If I _____ to detention, I _____ Sara. (go / meet)

3 If she _____ to my place, we _____ best friends. (come / become)

GET IT RIGHT!

would have + past participle

Learners sometimes underuse *would have* + past participle or use it in the *if*-clause where the past perfect tense is required.

✓ After the musical, we **would have gone** to a restaurant, but we didn't have time.

✗ After the musical, we ~~would go~~ to a restaurant, but we didn't have time.

✓ We would have appreciated it if you **had contacted** us.

✗ We would have appreciated it if you ~~would have contacted~~ us.

Circle the correct tense of the verb.

1 If I *would have to / had to* choose between the two schools, I would choose the larger one.

2 I *would have liked / 'd like* to visit, but I didn't have the chance.

3 It would have been better if we *had seen / would have seen* the other movie.

4 The food wasn't as tasty as I *would have liked / 'd like*.

5 If I'd known about the risks, I *wouldn't have agreed / would not agree* to go.

6 We could have learned more if the presentations *would have been / had been* better.

VOCABULARY

Being honest

bad
get away with (something)
hide the truth
tell a lie
lie
cheat

good
do the right thing
be open about (something)
tell the truth
own up (to something)

now

now (for the present)
now (for near future)
now that
now and then
just now

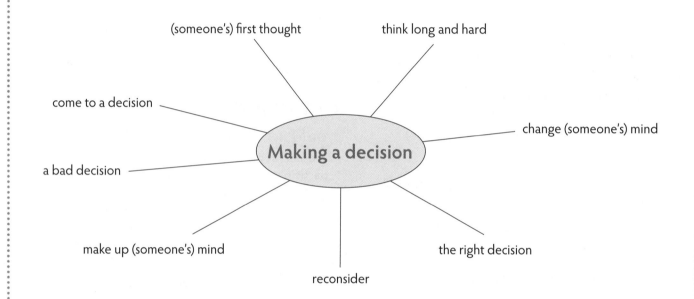

(someone's) first thought

think long and hard

come to a decision

change (someone's) mind

a bad decision

Making a decision

make up (someone's) mind

reconsider

the right decision

Key words in context

as soon as	I'll call you **as soon as** I know.
go-karting	Many racecar drivers start their careers **go-karting**.
helmet	You should always wear a **helmet** to protect your head when you ride a bike.
if	**If** you don't slow down, we're going to have an accident.
if only	**If only** I had a better computer! This one is so slow.
race	He won the **race** by more than 30 seconds.
reunite	The twins were separated when they were two years old and only **reunited** 20 years later.
unless	I won't say anything **unless** he asks me.
until	We waited **until** 10 and then went home.
when	**When** I got home, there was no one there.
wish	It's such a beautiful day. I **wish** I didn't have to work.

Being honest `SB page 40`

1 ★★☆ **Match the sentence halves.**

1 Why don't you just own ☐
2 I want to tell him the ☐
3 I can be very open ☐
4 I always find it really difficult to tell ☐
5 It's not always easy to do ☐
6 There's no point trying to hide ☐
7 She believed me! I never thought I'd get ☐
8 Liam's always trying to cheat ☐

a with my mom. We have a great relationship.
b the truth. People always find out.
c a lie. My face just gets bright red.
d away with that lie.
e on tests. He tries to look at my answers.
f the right thing, so thank you for being honest.
g up and tell her you broke her phone?
h truth, but I'm afraid he'll get angry.

2 ★★☆ **Complete the dialogue with the words in the list. There is one extra word.**

truth | honest | do | hide
own | cheat | lie | get

MANDY   So what do you think we should do?
        ¹_____ up and tell the ²_____ ?

RACHEL No way. She'll kill us. Let's ³_____ and
        say it wasn't us.

MANDY   We'll never ⁴_____ away with it. I think
        we have to ⁵_____ the right thing.

RACHEL Which is?

MANDY   Be ⁶_____ about it. Say we were hungry
        and there was nothing else to eat.

RACHEL But it was her birthday cake! She won't
        accept that as an excuse.

MANDY   So, what do you think we should do?

RACHEL ⁷_____ the truth. Say the dog ate it.

MANDY   The dog? That's great! Why didn't you
        suggest that earlier?

Making a decision `SB page 43`

3 ★★☆ **Match the expressions and the definitions.**

1 first thought ☐
2 to think long and hard ☐
3 to change your mind ☐
4 to reconsider ☐
5 to make up your mind ☐
6 a bad decision ☐

a to really consider something
b to think about your decision again
c to come to a decision
d not the right decision
e to come to a different decision
f original idea

4 ★★★ **Answer the questions.**

1 What were your first thoughts when you met your
  best friend?
  _____

2 What is the best decision you have ever made?
  _____

3 What is the worst decision you have ever made?
  _____

4 When do you find it difficult to make up your mind?
  _____

5 Think about a time when you changed your mind
  about something. What was it?
  _____

6 What kinds of things should a person think long
  and hard about?
  _____

WordWise `SB page 45`

now

5 ★★☆ **Rewrite the sentences with *now* in
the correct place.**

1 I go and see the local team play and then,
  but I'm not a huge fan.
  _____

2 John left just. If you run, you'll catch him.
  _____

3 We hardly ever see Lewis that he has his own
  phone.
  _____

4 We've missed the bus. What are we going
  to do?
  _____

READING

1 REMEMBER AND CHECK Put the events in the order that they happened. Then check your answers in the story on page 42 of the Student's Book.

a ☐ He receives money that helps him change his life.

b ☐ He remembers advice his grandfather once gave him.

c ☐ He meets Sarah.

d ☐ He sees his sisters for the first time in 16 years.

e ☐ He finds a ring in his cup.

f ☐ Billy hears a sound that is a little unusual.

g ☐ He refuses money that would help change his life.

h ☐ He shows the ring to an expert.

i ☐ He returns the ring to its rightful owner.

2 Read the article. What was the dilemma the game show contestants faced?

⊖ ☐ ✕   classicquizzes.com   ◄ ► ⌂

Golden Balls

A few years ago there was a game show on TV in which the contestants faced a really difficult dilemma. I can't really remember what happened in the show; I just remember how it finished. At the end there were two contestants, and they had the chance to win some money. Depending on how successful they'd been during the show, the amount of money could be from a few hundred dollars to well over $50,000. To get their hands on this money, they had to make one final decision.

In front of each of them were two balls that opened. One had the word "split" written inside; the other had the word "steal." If they wanted to share the money, they chose the "split" ball. If they wanted to keep all the money for themselves, they chose the "steal" ball. Each player chose a ball and then they showed it to each other at exactly the same time.

But it wasn't quite so simple. If they both chose the "split" ball, then they each went home with half the money. If one player chose the "split" ball while the other chose the "steal" ball, then the one who'd stolen went home with all the money, leaving the other player with no money at all. However, if they both chose the "steal" ball, then neither of them got any money at all.

Before they chose the ball, the players had a few minutes to tell each other what they were going to do.

Of course, they always promised they'd share, but they weren't always telling the truth. I remember always feeling really happy when the two players kept their promises and both went home with some money. It's always good to see the best side of people. Unfortunately, it didn't always end that way. When one player stole from the other, it made me feel really bad, especially when there was a lot of money involved. But the best feeling was when two greedy players both stole. It was great to see the look of disappointment on their faces when they realized they'd both thrown away the money.

The show revealed all sides of human nature, from the best to the worst. It only lasted a few years and then they stopped making it. I wonder why.

 posted July 19   1,425 views   SHARE

---

3 Read the article again and answer the questions.

There are two players, Sam and Jim. There is a total prize of $10,000.

How much does each player win in the situations below? How does the writer feel watching it?

1 They both choose the "split" ball.   Sam $_____   Jim $_____   Writer feels _____

2 They both choose the "steal" ball.   Sam $_____   Jim $_____   Writer feels _____

3 Jim chooses "split"; Sam chooses "steal."   Sam $_____   Jim $_____   Writer feels _____

4 Jim chooses "steal"; Sam chooses "split".   Sam $_____   Jim $_____   Writer feels _____

4 Imagine you are a contestant in the show. There is $10,000 to win. What would you do and why? Write a short paragraph.

DEVELOPING WRITING

A diary entry about a dilemma

1 Read the diary entry. What is Olivia's dilemma, and what does she decide to do?

> I have a confession to make. I haven't shown my best friend the trust she deserves, and I'm feeling really bad about it. It all started when she asked to borrow my tablet to check her email. Of course, I let her use it. [A] The problem is that she forgot to close it afterward, so when I went online a few hours later, her email page was the first thing I saw. I went to close it down when I noticed an email, a very unusual email. [B] but there it was — an email from my boyfriend to my best friend, and the title was my name — "Olivia!" I thought [1]_____. I knew I should just close the page, but I had to know: Why was he writing to her? I didn't even know he had her email address. I knew it was the [2]_____ to do, but I opened the message. [C] As soon as I read it, I knew I'd made a horrible mistake. The message was all about arranging a surprise party for my birthday at the end of the month.
>   Now I have a horrible dilemma. Should I [3]_____ and [4]_____ or say nothing and [5]_____ from her? If I was braver, I'd tell her what I'd done. [D] I think that this time I won't say anything and pretend that the party is a surprise. But I know there's one thing I'll never do again: I'll never let anyone use my tablet to check their email!

2 Complete the text with the phrases in the list. There is one extra phrase.

long and hard | tell a lie | tell her the truth | own up | wrong thing | hide the truth

3 These sentences have all been removed from the diary entry. Complete them using the verbs to make second or third conditionals. Then decide in which of the spaces (A–D) they go.

1   If I _____ (can turn) back time, I _____ (close) the page without taking a look. ☐

2   If I _____ (not see) it, I _____ (never think) of reading any of her messages. ☐

3   If I _____ (tell) her, she _____ (never speak) to me again. ☐

4   If I _____ just _____ (say) no, I _____ (not have) this dilemma. ☐

4 Read the dilemmas and then complete the conditional sentences.

1   *I broke my best friend's game console.*

   a   If I'd been more careful, _____

   b   If he knew it was me, _____

2   *I saw my best friend cheating on a test.*

   a   If I told the teacher, _____

   b   If my friend had studied harder, _____

3   *My friend wants to borrow $100 from me. It's all the money I have.*

   a   If I gave it to him and he never paid me back, _____

   b   If he had been more careful with his money, _____

5 Choose one of the dilemmas in Exercise 4 (or think of one of your own) and write a diary entry of about 250 words.

- Explain the dilemma.
- Explain the background behind the dilemma.
- Talk about what you should do.

CHECKLIST ✔

☐ Conditional sentences
☐ Honesty vocabulary
☐ Explanation of dilemma
☐ Background to dilemma
☐ Thoughts about what you should do

LISTENING

1 🔊 16 **Listen to the conversations. Match them with the pictures.**

2 🔊 16 **Listen again and complete the dialogues.**

Conversation 1

TEACHER Is there anything you'd like to tell me?

LIAM I d_____ k_____ w_____ to s_____ .

TEACHER You know this is a very serious offense.

LIAM I know, sir. I'm so a_____ .

Conversation 2

WOMAN My dress!

MAN Oh, I'm s_____ s_____ !

WOMAN It's OK. It's only water.

MAN I know, but it was so clumsy of me.

WOMAN D_____ w_____ a_____ it. Really. It's nothing.

Conversation 3

TINA But I haven't gotten you a present or even a card. I f_____ a_____ a_____ it.

LUCY No w_____ . It's fine.

DIALOGUE

Put the dialogue in the correct order.

a	1	TINA	Tell me it isn't your birthday today.
b		TINA	It isn't fine. I'm going right out and getting you something nice.
c		TINA	But I haven't gotten you a present or even a card. I feel awful about it.
d		TINA	What are you doing?
e		TINA	And tonight I'm taking you out for dinner. No argument.
f	13	TINA	Oh. I see. Well, next week then.
g		TINA	And I've forgotten it. I'm so embarrassed.
h		LUCY	Don't be silly. It's easy to do.
i		LUCY	No, seriously. You don't need to.
j		LUCY	It is. It's the big one – 40.
k		LUCY	No worries. It's fine.
l		LUCY	But I can't. I kind of have plans already.
m		LUCY	Well, it's just me and a few friends going out dancing.

PHRASES FOR FLUENCY SB page 45

1 **Complete the phrases with the missing vowels.**

1 _r_ y__ __t _f y__r m_nd?

2 b_l__v_ _t _r n_t

3 b_tw__n y__ _nd m_

4 _ w_s w_nd_r_ng _f

5 _ny ch_nc_?

6 wh_t's w_th

2 **Complete the conversations with the phrases from Exercise 1.**

1 A _____ the grumpy face, Ben? Life isn't so bad, is it?

   B No, I'm just a little tired. I didn't get a lot of sleep last night.

2 A I think we should take a break and play some tennis.

   B _____, I was thinking exactly the same thing. You read my mind!

3 A Um, Jen, I don't know if you're busy tonight, but _____ you'd like to go to the movies with me?

   B Sure! I'd love to!

4 A This room's a mess. Jack, _____ you could help me clean this up?

   B Sorry, Mom, but I'm busy playing Minecraft.

5 A That dog's really cute. I think we should take it home with us.

   B _____ It probably belongs to someone.

6 A Are you going to Yolanda's party?

   B _____, I don't really want to go. Her parties are always so boring.

> ## Pronunciation
> Consonant–vowel word linking
> **Go to page 119.**

Writing part 2

1 Look at the task. <u>Underline</u> the most important information in it.

WE ARE LOOKING FOR STORIES FOR A NEW WEBSITE FOR TEENAGERS.

Your story must start with the following sentence:
I opened the suitcase and could hardly believe my eyes; it was more money than I had ever seen in my life.

Your story must include:

- A decision
- A police officer

Write your story in 140–190 words.

2 Read Alan's answer. What does his story NOT include?

_____

I opened the suitcase and could hardly believe my eyes; it was more money than I had ever seen in my life. I closed it quickly and put the suitcase back onto the seat. I was excited, but I was also nervous – very nervous. I sat down next to it and thought about how this suitcase had fallen into my hands.

The woman had seemed normal. We started chatting, first about the weather and then about where we were going. She was on her way to visit her aunt. A man dressed in a dark suit passed by our seats. Her mood changed immediately. She seemed anxious and didn't want to talk. Then she got up suddenly. She asked me to watch the suitcase and left.

Two hours later, the train reached its final stop, the station where I was getting off. What was I going to do? Leave the money on the train or take it with me? I counted the money when I got home: $500,000 exactly. I used it to open a small store. Now, more than 20 years later, I have about 50 supermarkets across the whole country. I often think about that woman.

3 Look at the notes Alan made before he wrote his story. Use his story to answer the questions he asked himself.

1 Where was I?

_____

2 Why did I have this suitcase?

_____

3 How did I feel when I saw the money?

_____

4 What did I decide to do?

_____

5 What were the consequences?

_____

Exam guide: writing a story

In part 2 you have to answer one of four questions. You have a choice of an article, a review, an essay, an email/letter, or a story. It must be 140–190 words.

- Read the information carefully. Underline the important parts. Keep within the word limit. The starting sentence doesn't count in this total.
- Think carefully about who your reader is and why you are writing.
- Use the first sentence they give you to spark your imagination. Ask yourself questions like *"who?"*, *"why?"*, *"where?"*, and *"what next?"*.
- Think carefully about what kind of language you will use. When you write a story, you need to show a good use of the narrative tenses.
- Use descriptive language. Think carefully about the verbs, adjectives, and adverbs you use.
- Think about how you are going to link the sequence of events. Words like *as soon as*, *then*, *after that*, *before*, *after*, etc., will help you do this.

4 Read the task. Plan and then write your answer.

WE ARE LOOKING FOR STORIES FOR AN ENGLISH LANGUAGE MAGAZINE FOR TEENAGERS.

Your story must start with the following sentence:
Should I stay or should I go — I had 30 seconds to decide.

Your story must include:

- A dilemma
- A bike

Write your story in 140–190 words.

5 Ask a friend to read your story and complete the sentences about it.

I really like the _____

_____

I thought the story was _____

_____

The language you used well was _____

_____

You could improve it by _____

_____

CONSOLIDATION

LISTENING

1 🔊 19 Listen and (circle) A, B, or C.

1 The girl doesn't want the T-shirt because …
   - A it's too big.
   - B she doesn't like the color.
   - C she doesn't like the name on it.

2 The girl wants to exchange the T-shirt for …
   - A a belt.
   - B a different T-shirt.
   - C two other T-shirts.

3 The man suggests that the girl could …
   - A keep the T-shirt.
   - B give the T-shirt to her brother.
   - C give the T-shirt to someone else.

2 🔊 19 Listen again and mark the sentences T (true) or F (false).

1 The girl doesn't like clothes with the names of companies on them. ☐

2 All the clothes in the store have the company name on them. ☐

3 The T-shirt was a present from the girl's brother. ☐

4 The shirt has a hole in it. ☐

5 The girl doesn't have the receipt. ☐

6 The belt is more expensive than the T-shirt. ☐

7 The girl is bigger than her friend Jenny. ☐

8 She decides to give the T-shirt to her friend. ☐

VOCABULARY

3 Match the sentences.

1 Everyone knows who she is. ☐
2 She's traveled all over the world. ☐
3 She's totally honest. ☐
4 She just doesn't know what to do. ☐
5 She stuck with her original decision. ☐
6 She doesn't want to use her real name. ☐

a She can't make up her mind at all.
b She didn't want to change her mind.
c So she's decided to use a stage name.
d She's a household name in this country.
e I've never heard her tell a lie.
f You name it, she's been there!

4 (Circle) the correct options.

1 I haven't decided yet. I'm going to think long and *hard / strong* about it.

2 We haven't gone there very often since we moved – just *now that / now and then*.

3 Come on, tell us the *lie / truth* about what happened.

4 I know you did it. Come on, it isn't important. You should just *get away with it / own up to it*.

5 I really don't care if people make fun of me or *make me / call me* names.

6 I think you've made the wrong decision. If you want to *reconsider / come to a decision*, please call me.

7 I don't like the *logo / brand* of this company. It's not very well designed.

8 He's the owner of a big *chain / brand* of shoe stores in the northern part of the country.

GRAMMAR

5 Correct the sentences.

1 I wish you are here.

_____

2 I was happier if the weather was better.

_____

3 If only I know the answer to this question.

_____

4 We'd better to leave now, I think.

_____

5 I'll call you when I'll get home.

_____

6 Do you think we should asking for some help?

_____

7 He's a great guitar player – if only he can sing better.

_____

8 If he'd left earlier, he hadn't missed the start of the movie.

_____

9 The bus ride there is free, so you have to pay for it.

_____

10 Let's wait as soon as 5 p.m. to call them.

_____

DIALOGUE

6 **Complete the dialogue with the phrases in the list.**

I was wondering | any chance
are you out of your mind | had better
should be | believe it or not
what's with | between you and me

LEAH Hey, Jim. ¹_____
if you're going to Lucy's party later.

JIM Yeah, I'm going. Why?

LEAH ²_____ I can go with you?
I don't like arriving at parties on my own.

JIM Sure, no problem.

LEAH That's great. Thanks. Hey, you'll never guess what happened to me in a store this morning.

JIM What happened?

LEAH Well, I bought a really cool shirt for the party tonight. ³_____, it was $79.99! I can't believe I spent so much!

JIM Wow, that's really expensive. But so what?

LEAH Well, you know, my parents gave me some money for my birthday, so I paid cash with two $50 bills. I put them on the counter, and the woman saw them, so she turned around to ring it up and get my change. Then, ⁴_____, the woman put the change on top of the $50 bills! I picked it all up and left. So I got the shirt and my money and the change! How cool is that?

JIM Cool? ⁵_____? It's dishonest. Think about the poor sales assistant. She'll probably have to pay that money back out of her own pocket. You ⁶_____ take it back and explain. Say it was a mistake.

LEAH No way. She ⁷_____ more careful.

JIM Whatever. I'm sure you wouldn't like it if you were that woman.

LEAH Oh come on, Jim. ⁸_____ you? Don't be so boring.

JIM Boring? Leah, what you did was stealing, you know?

SPAM

Back in 1937 there was a company in the U.S. that made a kind of meat that was in a can. There was a contest among the employees to give this canned meat a name. The winner won $100 for inventing the name: Spam. (Some people think the name was made from the words "spiced ham.") Spam became very popular during World War II in Europe when it was a very important food item. Spam is still made today and sold around the world.

Interesting things have happened to the name. In the 1970s there was a famous comedy show on British TV that did a sketch about a café where everything on the menu had Spam in it. They even invented a song that is mainly the word "Spam" sung over and over again. By doing this the comedians created the idea that Spam was everywhere, that you couldn't avoid it, and no one really wanted it. More than 20 years later, when email began, people started receiving lots of unwanted emails. They were everywhere, and you couldn't avoid them. And what is that kind of email called? Why, spam, of course.

The company that makes Spam (the meat, that is) was not too happy about this use of the name and tried for many years to find a way to stop it. But finally they gave up. Now Spam is both things.

READING

7 **Read the online article. Answer the questions.**

1 What is one possible meaning of the name "Spam"?
_____

2 When and where was Spam an important food?
_____

3 What idea did the comedy show create about Spam?
_____

4 Why is unwanted email called "spam"?
_____

5 How did the meat manufacturer feel about emails being called spam?
_____

WRITING

8 **Think of two products you know – one that you like the name of and one that you don't like the name of. Write a paragraph (100–120 words). Include this information:**

● what the products are and what they do
● what their names are
● why you like / dislike the names (the sound? the meaning of the name? the way the name is written? another reason?)

5 WHAT A STORY!

GRAMMAR
Relative pronouns `SB page 50`

1 ★☆☆ Complete the sentences with *who, whose, where, that,* or *which.*

1 The book _____ I just read is called *Clockwork Angel.*

2 It is a fantasy novel _____ was written by Cassandra Clare.

3 The name of the girl _____ is the heroine of the novel is Tessa Gray.

4 The story is set in London, _____ all the action takes place.

5 Tessa Gray is looking for her brother, _____ has disappeared.

6 Tessa gets help from two friends _____ names are Will and Jem.

Defining and non-defining relative clauses `SB page 50`

2 ★★☆ Combine the sentences about a famous vampire with *who, which, where, that,* or *whose.*

0 Abhartach was a vampire. He came from Ireland.
   Abhartach was a vampire who came from Ireland.

1 It was a legend. It inspired Bram Stoker to write *Dracula.*
   _____

2 Abhartach was an evil magician. He had very strong powers.
   _____

3 He lived in Derry. He ruled a small kingdom.
   _____

4 He was an evil ruler. His people were afraid of him.
   _____

5 *Dracula* comes from an Irish word. It means bad blood.
   _____

3 ★★☆ Complete the conversation with *which, who, that, where,* or *whose.*

HOLLY What kind of books do you like reading?

ANNA I like reading books [1]_____ have vampires or witches in them. My favorite book is one about a girl [2]_____ grandmother was a witch. It's a historical novel [3]_____ is about a witch.

HOLLY Is it set in England?

ANNA No, it's set in the U.S. [4]_____ Mary, "the witch girl," is sent after her grandmother's death. What about you? What kind of books do you like?

HOLLY I like historical novels. I'm reading one now [5]_____ is set in Victorian England. It's about a poor girl [6]_____ has to work. She works for a famous medium, Madam Savoya, [7]_____ job is to contact the spirits of dead people for their relatives.

ANNA It sounds like the kind of book [8]_____ I'd like to read. Can I borrow it when you're finished?

4 ★★☆ Put the words in the correct order to make sentences with non-defining relative clauses.

1 daughter, / My / lives / in / Madrid, / who / an / author / is
   _____

2 movie, / The / stars / Helen Weaver, / which / out / on / DVD / is / now
   _____

3 storyteller, / The / work / all / over / the / world, / whose / takes / him / in / Japan / is / now / right
   _____

4 Prague, / where / boy / the / story / the / in / grew up, / my / hometown / is
   _____

5 heroine / story, / the / of / The / whose / father / French, / is / named / Sophie / is
   _____

5 ★★☆ Write D (defining) or N (non-defining) next to the relative clauses.

1 My favorite book, which is about a vampire, has just been made into a movie. ☐

2 The boy, who had also read the book, liked the movie more. ☐

3 The man who she's interviewing wrote the book. ☐

4 I couldn't find any travel literature on Morocco, where I'm going on vacation next month. ☐

5 My aunt, who is a poet, lives in Rio. ☐

6 The girl whose father was rescued in the story was Spanish. ☐

7 The fairy tale, which was written in the 19th century, is still popular today. ☐

8 I couldn't watch the horror movie that was on TV last night. ☐

6 ★★★ Rewrite the sentences with *who*, *which*, *where*, *that*, or *whose* and the clauses in parentheses.

0 The girl had long red hair. (mother is the heroine of the story)
   The girl, whose mother is the heroine of the story, had long red hair.

1 The city is my hometown. (all the action took place)

2 The park is the scene of the crime. (the murdered woman's body was found)

3 The story is very sad. (is set in a future world)

4 The villain was in fact a good man. (was killed at the end of the story)

5 The crime was never solved. (was committed at the beginning of the story)

Relative clauses with *which* [SB page 53]

7 ★★☆ Read the sentence pairs. In your notebook, write a new (third) sentence that has the same meaning as the sentence pair. Use *which*.

0 My parents used to read lots of stories to me when I was a child. I enjoyed this a lot.
   My parents used to read lots of stories to me when I was a child, which I enjoyed a lot.

1 Their train arrived four hours late. This meant they missed the show.

2 None of my friends had studied for the test. This made their parents really angry.

3 Most of my friends don't like the new Pixar movie. I can't understand this.

8 ★★★ Complete the sentences so they are true for you.

1 One of my friends _____, which is very good news.

2 Lots of people on my street _____, which I find annoying.

3 Not many people want to _____, which I think is a shame.

GET IT RIGHT! 👁

that vs. *which* in relative clauses

Learners sometimes mistakenly use *that* in non-defining relative clauses.

We usually use *that* in defining relative clauses.

✓ This is the solution **that** you are looking for.

We only use *which* in non-defining relative clauses.

✓ I'm in Brazil, **which** is a beautiful country.

✗ I'm in Brazil, ~~that~~ is a beautiful country.

Check (✓) the sentences that are better with *that* in. Write an ✗ for those that should use *which*.

1 I spent $100, (which / that) is too much. ☐

2 I want a car (which / that) can go fast. ☐

3 Pete has a computer (which / that) has some good games on it. ☐

4 We should buy the one (which / that) is cheaper. ☐

5 I won't be there, (which / that) is a problem. ☐

6 The basement door was left open all night, (which / that) is very unsafe ☐

7 The class (which / that) the drama students liked most was, surprisingly, history. ☐

8 Flowers (which / that) bloom early in the spring don't last as long as summer bloomers. ☐

VOCABULARY

Types of stories

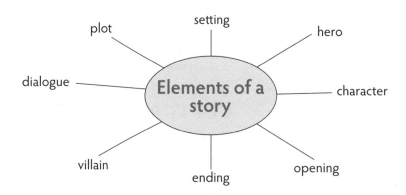

Key words in context

adolescent	Young adult fiction is aimed at **adolescents**, but adults often enjoy it, too.
anecdote	I love listening to **anecdotes** that people tell about traveling.
blockbuster	This movie will become a **blockbuster**. I'm sure it will make more money than *Avatar*.
capture (one's) attention	The story was so dramatic, it **captured everyone's attention**.
engage	If a book doesn't **engage** my interest from the beginning, I usually don't finish reading it.
fairy tale	I loved listening to **fairy tales** when I was a child.
influential	This theory has been **influential** for many years.
inspiration	Her story of overcoming problems has been an **inspiration** to many people.
memorize	When my parents went to school, they frequently had to **memorize** long texts.
original	The **original** story comes from Africa, I think.
pass down	This story has been **passed down** from generation to generation.
potential	This is a great book. It has the **potential** to be turned into a movie.
revisit	Have you ever **revisited** the stories from your childhood?
romance	The **romance** between the main characters grows throughout the book.
special effects	I thought the movie wasn't great, but the **special effects** were awesome.
tradition	Ireland is a country with a rich **tradition** of storytelling.

Types of stories SB page 51

1 ★☆☆ **Match the descriptions of the books to their genres.**

1 poetry ☐
2 horror story ☐
3 short stories ☐
4 autobiography ☐
5 romantic novel ☐
6 historical novel ☐
7 travel literature ☐
8 crime novel ☐
9 science fiction ☐

a *War Horse* by Michael Morpurgo is set during World War I. Albert's father sells his horse Joey to the army, and he goes into battle in France.

b In *Noughts and Crosses*, by Malorie Blackman, Sephy is a cross and Callum is a nought. They fall in love, but in their world noughts and crosses shouldn't be friends. Like Romeo and Juliet, their love is forbidden.

c *Jump Ball: A Basketball Season in Poems* by Mel Glenn. Through a series of poems we get to know the members of a school basketball team.

d *Fahrenheit 451* by Ray Bradbury is about a future world where books are not allowed. All books are burned by "firemen," whose job it is to start fires.

e *The Boy Who Biked the World* is by a cyclist, Alastair Humphreys, who completed a bicycle trip around the world in four years. The story follows a boy's bicycle trip through Europe and Africa.

f *Boy: Tales of Childhood* by Roald Dahl is about the author's childhood in Norway and his life at an English boarding school.

g *Haunted* by R.L. Stine is about a girl who is visited by a ghost from the future. Together they try to stop the death of a boy from occurring. Sometimes it's really scary.

h *Whodunit? Detective Stories*, edited by Philip Pullman, is a collection of detective stories by famous authors.

i In *The London Eye Mystery* by Siobhan Dowd, Ted and Kat's cousin Salim gets on the London Eye, but he never gets off again. Ted and Kat follow the clues across London to help the police find their cousin.

Elements of a story SB page 53

2 ★★☆ **Complete the dialogue with the words in the list.**

characters | ending | villain | plot | setting | hero

HARRY OK, ask me questions and try to guess the book I'm thinking of.

MIKE Right. Where does the action take place?

HARRY The ¹_____ for the story is London in Victorian England.

MIKE What's it about?

HARRY The ²_____ follows the life of a man in the past, the present, and the future. The ³_____ of the book is a very mean man, but he sees his faults, and he changes. Three of the ⁴_____ are ghosts.

MIKE Who's the bad character then? Who's the ⁵_____ ?

HARRY There isn't one.

MIKE And does it have a happy ⁶_____ ?

HARRY Yes, it does.

MIKE I think it's *A Christmas Carol* by Charles Dickens.

HARRY Good guess! You're right. Now it's your turn.

3 ★★★ **Now complete the dialogue about a story (or a movie) that you like.**

MIKE Where does the action take place?

ME The _____ for the story is _____ .

MIKE What's it about?

ME The _____ .

MIKE Who is the hero or heroine of the book?

ME _____ .

MIKE Who's the bad character then? Who's the _____ ?

ME _____ .

MIKE And does it have a happy _____ ?

ME _____ .

MIKE I think it's _____ by _____ .

4 ★★☆ **Complete the sentences with the words in the list.**

blockbuster | influential | tradition
romance | anecdotes | special effects

1 Nelson Mandela's very _____ book, *A Long Walk to Freedom*, made people aware of the inequalities between people.

2 The two main characters fall in love, and the movie follows their _____ .

3 She tells lots of funny _____ about her family.

4 The novel, which was very successful, was made into a _____ movie.

5 It was a science fiction story, so the movie had lots of cool _____ .

6 Our family has a _____ of telling stories on Christmas Day.

READING

1 REMEMBER AND CHECK **Answer the questions. Then check your answers in the article on page 49 of the Student's Book.**

1 What does the writer say most people think of when they hear the word "storytelling?"

_____

2 What forms of storytelling are mentioned?

_____

3 How did the Neanderthal man in the story die?

_____

4 What else do stories do other than just entertain us?

_____

5 How did storytellers find new stories?

_____

6 What do our stories reflect?

_____

2 **Read the article quickly. What is the profession of the "star" in the picture? Circle the answer.**

A singer   B actor   C author   D politician

3 **Read the article again. Mark the sentences T (true) or F (false). Then correct the false sentences.**

1 Charles Dickens toured England and Europe as a storyteller. ☐

_____

2 Charles Dickens lived nearly 200 years ago. ☐

_____

3 He earned a lot of money for his first performance of *A Christmas Carol*. ☐

_____

4 In those days a lot of people couldn't read. ☐

_____

5 His family wanted him to stop touring because his readings weren't popular. ☐

_____

6 The train car that Charles Dickens was in fell down a steep slope. ☐

_____

7 After the accident Charles Dickens was scared of traveling by train. ☐

_____

8 Charles Dickens died of a heart attack in 1870. ☐

_____

A star is born!

Thousands of people came to the theaters and concert halls to hear him. Performances were sold out in the U.K. and the United States. People fainted at his shows. Who do you think he was? Well, he wasn't a rock star. He was in fact a writer, and he didn't live in this century. He lived nearly 200 years ago. Maybe you have heard of him or read one of his books? His name is Charles Dickens.

In the 19th century Charles Dickens went on long tours in the U.K. and the U.S. At each performance he read and acted out passages from his novels. These reading tours were very popular, and they brought him fame and fortune.

Why did he go on tour with his books? His first tour was for charity – he wasn't paid for it. The first performance was of *A Christmas Carol* for 2,000 poor people in Birmingham, England. Many people in the audience couldn't read, so storytelling was very important to them. After this first performance he was offered money to perform his readings in other places. At first he refused, but later he agreed to do more shows. He loved performing, and as a young man he had wanted to be an actor. His tour of the U.S. from December 1867 to April 1868 earned him more than £19,000, which was a huge amount of money at the time. It was a lot more than he earned from selling his books.

Charles Dickens' tours were very hard work because he traveled long distances by train, and trains were very slow in those days. His family and friends became worried about his health. They wanted him to stop touring.

In 1865 there was a terrible train crash at Staplehurst in England. All the train cars except one fell down a steep slope. What happened to Charles Dickens? He was in the one train car that didn't go down the slope. After the accident Charles Dickens was frightened of traveling by train, but he still continued his tours. His readings continued to be successful.

However, his friends and family were right to be worried about his health. Five years later, in 1870, Charles Dickens died of a stroke.

He is still very popular today, and millions of people around the world read his books.

4 **If you could watch any "star" perform live, who would it be? Write a short paragraph and give reasons for your choice.**

DEVELOPING WRITING

A book review

1 Match the sentence halves.

1 The hero or heroine of the book ☐
2 The setting ☐
3 The opening sentence ☐
4 It is very important to have a strong ending ☐
5 Some writers include jokes and witty dialogue, ☐
6 There may be several different characters ☐

a at the beginning of the book is very important.
b which make the story more entertaining.
c that satisfies the reader.
d is the person who is the main character.
e is where the action takes place.
f who have different strengths and weaknesses.

2 Look at the book cover. What genre of story is it? Circle the answer.

A horror story   B travel adventure   C poetry
D romantic novel   E science fiction

3 Answer the questions about the book review.

Paragraph 1

1 What is the story about in general? (Write about the plot but don't give the whole plot or the ending away.)

2 Where does the story take place? (Give the setting.)

Paragraph 2

3 What happened to Tom, the main character, that the writer can identify with?

4 Did the writer like the book? What was his / her favorite thing about it?

Paragraph 3

5 Does the writer recommend the book to older readers, younger readers, or all ages?

6 How does the reader rate the book? What are his / her reasons?

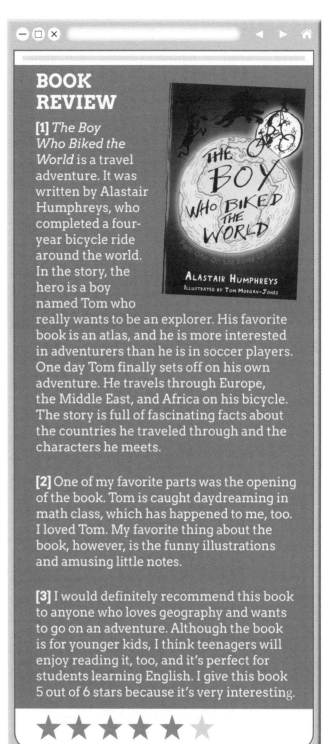

BOOK REVIEW

[1] *The Boy Who Biked the World* is a travel adventure. It was written by Alastair Humphreys, who completed a four-year bicycle ride around the world. In the story, the hero is a boy named Tom who really wants to be an explorer. His favorite book is an atlas, and he is more interested in adventurers than he is in soccer players. One day Tom finally sets off on his own adventure. He travels through Europe, the Middle East, and Africa on his bicycle. The story is full of fascinating facts about the countries he traveled through and the characters he meets.

[2] One of my favorite parts was the opening of the book. Tom is caught daydreaming in math class, which has happened to me, too. I loved Tom. My favorite thing about the book, however, is the funny illustrations and amusing little notes.

[3] I would definitely recommend this book to anyone who loves geography and wants to go on an adventure. Although the book is for younger kids, I think teenagers will enjoy reading it, too, and it's perfect for students learning English. I give this book 5 out of 6 stars because it's very interesting.

★★★★★☆

4 Now choose a book to review. Use the review and the questions above to help you plan your writing. Then write a short review of the book in 200 words.

CHECKLIST ✔

☐ Use adjectives to make your review more interesting
☐ Use *that, which, who, whose,* and *where* to improve your writing style

LISTENING

1 🔊20 **Read the sentences below. Then listen and write the numbers of the conversations (1, 2, or 3).**

a   He sees three players from his favorite baseball team. ☐

b   She sees a famous actor whose name she has forgotten. ☐

c   She sees a friend of a friend that she hasn't seen for months. ☐

d   He was in a restaurant, where he was having a meal with his family. ☐

e   She was in a bookstore, where she was buying a book for her brother. ☐

f   She was shopping on a Saturday. ☐

2 🔊20 **Listen again and mark the sentences T (true) or F (false).**

1   Katie saw her best friend in the bookstore. ☐

2   Amanda sometimes thinks of somebody, and then they call or text her. ☐

3   Jake's team won the soccer game on Saturday. ☐

4   Jake saw three New York Cosmos players in a restaurant. ☐

5   Sarah was shopping downtown when she saw a famous actor. ☐

6   The annoying thing is that Sarah can't remember the actor's address. ☐

DIALOGUE

1 Put the words in order.

1   never / what / believe / You'll / happened

_____

2   strangest / me / to / happened / thing / The

_____

3   me / finish / Let

_____

4   the / That's / annoying / thing

_____

5   the / are / chances / What

_____ ?

6   strange / What's / that / about

_____ ?

2 Put the dialogue in the correct order.

a ☐ MIKE   Well, I haven't seen her for a long time, but yesterday I was thinking about her. And then this morning I saw her. What are the chances, huh?

b ☐ MIKE   Yes. And that's the annoying thing – you're always right!

c 1 MIKE   The strangest thing happened to me this morning. I saw that girl Louise downtown!

d ☐ MIKE   Yes, she does, but …

e ☐ SANDY   Let me finish. And she works in a store downtown, too. So it isn't strange at all. Am I right?

f ☐ SANDY   You saw Louise? What's strange about that?

g ☐ SANDY   The chances are really good, actually. I mean, she lives here, doesn't she? And …

3 Complete the conversation with a word from the list. There is one extra word.

annoying | believe | chances | finish
happened | strange | strangest

MARIA   You'll never ¹_____ what happened last night. That movie *Ghost* was on TV! It was just the ²_____ thing!

PAUL   Why? What's ³_____ about that? They show *Ghost* on TV a lot.

MARIA   Let me ⁴_____. You see, I wanted to watch it on Sunday. I found the DVD at home, but the ⁵_____ thing was that it didn't work anymore.

PAUL   I hate it when a DVD stops working.

MARIA   But then the next day, I turned the TV on, and there it was! What are the ⁶_____ of that?

PAUL   That is a little strange.

Pronunciation
/ə/ in word endings
Go to page 119.   🔊

Reading and Use of English part 5

Exam guide: multiple choice

In this part of the exam you will read a text followed by six multiple-choice questions. Each correct answer receives two points.

- Read the whole text before looking at the questions.
- Read all the questions and leave the ones you are not sure about until the end.
- When you have finished the easy questions, go back to any questions you are unsure about. Ask yourself, "What answers are not possible?" Eliminate the wrong or impossible answers first.

You are going to read a review of Jules Verne's classic novel, *Around the World in 80 Days*. For questions 1–6, choose the answer (A, B, C, or D) that you think fits best according to the text.

Jules Verne's novel, *Around the World in 80 Days*, has inspired many people to travel around the world in unusual ways. It has also inspired several movies, TV shows, theater productions, and even a board game.

So where did Jules Verne get the idea for his book? He told a reporter that he had been sitting in a café in Paris one day when he saw a newspaper advertisement for the very first tourist trip around the world in 1872.

In Jules Verne's story, a wealthy English gentleman, Phileas Fogg, accepts a bet of £20,000 that he can travel around the world in 80 days. Phileas Fogg is a man who is very hard to please. For example, he fires his servant because the servant brings him some water to wash with that is 29°C instead of 30°C. He has a very strict routine, and he follows it to the letter every day.

Fogg employs a new servant, Passepartout, and on Wednesday, October 2, 1872, they set off on a journey around the world. While he's in India, Fogg falls in love with an Indian girl, Aouda. The journey ends back in London with Fogg believing that he has arrived a day too late and that he has lost the bet. He tells Aouda that he cannot marry her now because he's too poor. Passepartout learns that they have gotten the date wrong. The party traveled from east to west, so they gained a day. Fogg hurries to his club and arrives there in time to win the bet, and the story ends happily.

The story is an easy read. The humorous twists and turns of the plot keep you entertained throughout. It is a romantic adventure story that I would highly recommend to all my friends.

1 What does the reviewer explain in the first paragraph?
   A The story inspired people of Phileas Fogg's generation to travel.
   B The story gave people the idea of trying to travel around the world in different ways.
   C The story inspired adventurers around the world to draw maps of their travels.
   D The story inspired adventurers to navigate ships around the world.

2 What gave Jules Verne the idea for the story?
   A He had just returned from an interesting trip around the world.
   B He had seen a movie about a trip around the world.
   C He had seen a play about an around-the-world vacation.
   D He saw an advertisement for a trip around the world.

3 What does the reviewer mean by "he follows it to the letter"?
   A Phileas Fogg writes a letter about his routine every day.
   B He follows a routine that is written in a letter.
   C He has written his valet a letter about his routine.
   D He follows exactly the same routine every day.

4 Why does Phileas Fogg employ a new servant?
   A His old servant brings him water that is too hot.
   B His old servant makes one little mistake.
   C His old servant is always making mistakes.
   D His new servant charges less money.

5 Why can't Phileas Fogg marry Aouda?
   A He has fallen in love with another girl.
   B He is already married.
   C He thinks he doesn't have enough money to marry.
   D He thinks he has lost the bet so he has to set off on another journey.

6 What is the reviewer's opinion of the book?
   A The book is a fun story filled with adventure and romance that everybody will enjoy reading.
   B The book is only entertaining for people who like romance novels.
   C The book has a very serious message about world travel for readers of all ages.
   D The reviewer recommends that you read the book before setting off on a long journey.

6 HOW DO THEY DO IT?

GRAMMAR
Present and past passive (review)
SB page 58

1 ★☆☆ (Circle) the correct option.

1 The best sports cars *make / are made* in Italy.

2 The concert *showed / was shown* live on TV.

3 She *texts / is texted* me at least five times a day.

4 The 2012 Olympics *held / were held* in London.

5 My dad *makes / is made* model trains as a hobby.

6 Letters *deliver / aren't delivered* on Sundays.

7 Jacob's really good at tennis. He *coaches / is coached* by his mom.

8 A 63-year-old woman *won / was won* the talent show.

2 ★★☆ Complete with the past passive forms of the verbs.

The school magic show was a big success. All the tickets ⁰ *were sold* (sell), and some amazing tricks ¹_____ (perform) by three very talented magicians. Here are some of my favorites: The principal ²_____ (saw) in half. A piece of paper ³_____ (turn) into hundreds of butterflies. Coins ⁴_____ (find) behind the ears of a student, and of course, a rabbit ⁵_____ (pull) out of a hat.

3 ★★★ Write questions in the present or past passive using the prompts.

0 President Kennedy / shoot

When *was President Kennedy shot?*

1 Mona Lisa / paint Leonardo da Vinci

When _____

2 the first helicopter / build

When _____

3 BMWs / make

Where _____

4 The Oscars / hold every year

Where _____

5 2014 World Cup final / play

Where _____

4 ★★★ Write answers to the questions in Exercise 3. Use the clues in the list to help you.

Germany | Rio de Janeiro | 1963
Los Angeles | 1936 | around 1503

0 *He was shot in 1963.*

1 _____

2 _____

3 _____

4 _____

5 _____

have something done
SB page 59

5 ★★☆ Read about the hotel and then complete the letter.

Welcome to the
Ritz Hotel!

We have everything you need for the perfect weekend.

0 We park your car on arrival.

1 We take your bags to your room.

2 A top chef cooks all your meals.

3 Room service brings your meals to your room.

4 We deliver tickets to top shows to your room.

5 We wash and iron all your clothes.

6 A top stylist cuts your hair for free.

We had a wonderful weekend at the Ritz Hotel.

0 *We had our car parked for us when we arrived.*

1 _____

2 _____

3 _____

4 _____

5 _____

6 _____

6 ★★★ What did these people have done yesterday? Write sentences.

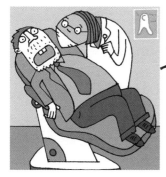

0 teeth / check

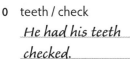
He had his teeth checked.

1 hair / dye

_____

_____

2 pizza / deliver

_____

_____

3 washing machine / fix

_____

_____

Future and present perfect passive
SB page 61

7 ★☆☆ Complete the text with the words in the list.

haven't been painted | will be sold | will be shown
will be finished | has been made | will be put up
have been built | haven't been widened

The Olympic Games open here soon, but is the city ready? All the stadiums ¹_____, but many of them ²_____ yet. The builders promise that they ³_____ before the opening day. The city airport ⁴_____ bigger, but the roads from the airport into the city ⁵_____, so traffic will be a huge problem. Most of the tickets have been sold already, and the organizers believe all of them ⁶_____ in the next few weeks. So make sure you get yours soon. Big screens ⁷_____ around the city, and many events ⁸_____ live on them, so you can also enjoy the amazing Olympic atmosphere in our beautiful city.

8 ★★☆ Complete the sentences with the present perfect passive form of the verbs.

1 The windows are really dirty. They _____ (not clean) for months.
2 Have you heard the news? The bank robbers _____ (catch).
3 The test _____ (grade). You can find out your score online.
4 We've been waiting for an hour, and our pizza still _____ (not deliver).
5 Hey! Your bill _____ (not pay) yet.

9 ★★★ Rewrite the sentences using the passive.

1 They'll play the final game on Thursday.
   _____
2 They won't pay me until next month.
   _____
3 A famous scientist will deliver the report.
   _____
4 They've closed the hospital.
   _____
5 The earthquake has destroyed the whole city.
   _____
6 No one has seen them for days.
   _____

GET IT RIGHT!
Future passive

Learners sometimes use the wrong tense where the future passive is required or use the future passive where it is not required.

✓ The changes **will be introduced** next year.
✗ The changes will introduce next year.
✗ The changes are introduced next year.

Correct the errors in the sentences.

1 This money will use to develop the city.
   _____
2 In the future the population will be increased.
   _____
3 If the concert doesn't start soon, we are forced to leave.
   _____
4 Please see the questionnaire that will be enclosed with this letter.
   _____
5 The show will host on Friday at 10 a.m.
   _____

VOCABULARY

Make and do

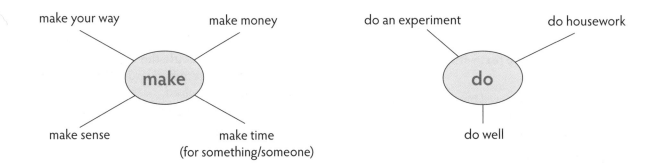

Key words in context

apparently	**Apparently** that trick is done with mirrors. I'm not sure exactly how though.
concerned	Tim's teacher is a bit **concerned** about him. She thinks he's not working as hard as he used to.
disbelief	There was a look of **disbelief** on her face as if she'd seen a ghost.
fake	It's not a real Picasso. It's a **fake**.
float	The magician made the lady **float** up into the air.
illusion	The lady didn't really disappear. It was just a clever **illusion**.
onlooker	**Onlookers** watched in horror as the two men robbed the old lady in the middle of the street.
spectator	There were more than 30,000 **spectators** at the final game.
support	One corner of the table is **supported** by a pile of books.

Extreme adjectives and modifiers
SB page 58

1 ★☆☆ **Find nine extreme adjectives in the word search and write them next to the non-extreme adjectives.**

G	R	E	A	T	T	L	U	F	W	A
N	P	G	B	E	N	I	B	V	W	D
I	Y	A	Q	R	A	K	C	G	J	E
T	T	E	F	R	I	O	O	K	E	L
A	V	T	C	I	Y	P	E	P	N	I
N	W	U	O	B	L	N	L	B	O	G
I	G	N	I	L	I	O	B	C	R	H
C	R	I	I	E	R	F	O	P	M	T
S	U	M	N	I	B	E	F	K	O	E
A	A	B	L	I	H	Y	T	F	U	D
F	A	N	T	A	S	T	I	C	S	D

interesting ¹_____

happy ²_____

big ³_____

good (x2) ⁴_____ ⁵_____

bad (x2) ⁶_____ ⁷_____

hot ⁸_____

small ⁹_____

2 ★★☆ **Complete the sentences with extreme or ordinary adjectives.**

1 The play wasn't funny; it was absolutely
   h_____.

2 Their new baby isn't s_____; it's really tiny.

3 Our vacation wasn't just good; it was w_____.

4 I wasn't s_____; I was absolutely terrified.

5 Dad isn't sad; he's really m_____.

6 It's not c_____ outside; it's absolutely freezing.

7 The new shopping center isn't big; it's absolutely
   h_____.

8 The rollercoaster ride wasn't e_____; it was
   thrilling.

9 The book wasn't i_____; it was fascinating.

10 They weren't just g_____; they were amazing!

3 ★★☆ **Choose the correct word, a or b. If both are possible choose c (both).**

1 We spent our vacation in Brazil, and it was _____
   boiling.
   a very **b** absolutely **c** both

2 Have you seen their house? It's _____
   enormous!
   a very **b** absolutely **c** both

3 I liked the movie. I thought it was _____ funny.
   a very **b** absolutely **c** both

4 Put a coat on. It's _____ cold outside.
   a very **b** really **c** both

5 I think the idea of time travel is _____ fascinating.
   a very **b** absolutely **c** both

6 She's an artist. Her paintings are _____ good.
   a very **b** really **c** both

make and *do* SB page 61

4 ★☆☆ **Complete the sentences with *make* or *do*.**

1 It just doesn't _____ any sense to me.

2 There must be easier ways to _____ money.

3 Maybe it's time to _____ some housework.

4 Can you _____ your own way? I'm a little busy at
   the moment.

5 I don't usually _____ this kind of experiment,
   but I don't see what can go wrong.

6 Jack's been pretty lonely since his best friend moved
   away. We should _____ time to see him this
   weekend.

5 ★★☆ **Match the sentences in Exercise 4 with the pictures.**

READING

1 ` REMEMBER AND CHECK ` Match the places and the events. Then check your answers in the article on page 57 of the Student's Book.

1 ☐ Central London
2 ☐ The banks of the River Thames
3 ☐ On the River Thames
4 ☐ Bradford
5 ☐ New Orleans

a Crowds watch a man walk out onto the river.
b Dynamo's home town.
c Dynamo gets into a police boat.
d Dynamo falls in love with magic.
e Dynamo waves to crowds from a bus.

2 Read the article. What is the name of his performance in the picture? _____

HOW DOES HE DO IT?

When American magician David Blaine started his professional career, people were soon talking about the originality of his shows. However, David had more ambitious plans and started a series of amazing public performances, each designed to push his body further and further to its limits. Here are a few:

BURIED ALIVE

In April 1999 David performed his first major public stunt. For seven days he was buried underground in a tiny plastic box in New York. A large tank of water was placed on top of the box, and the only way he could communicate was with a handheld electric buzzer. He ate nothing and drank just three tablespoons of water a day. Around 75,000 people visited the site to see David.

ABOVE THE BELOW

In September 2003 David took his show to Europe. For 44 days he lived in a transparent plastic box that was hung nine meters in the air on the banks of the River Thames in London. During this time, he ate nothing and drank just four and a half liters of water a day. A webcam inside the box filmed the whole event live. The large crowds that came to watch were not always kind; they threw objects such as eggs, bottles, and golf balls. When he came out of the box, David was taken straight to the hospital because he was very weak from eating nothing.

DROWNED ALIVE

In May 2006 David climbed into a large globe filled with water, which was to be his home for the next week. All that connected him to the outside world were two tubes, one for air and the other to provide food. To finish the performance, David planned to try to break the world record for holding one's breath under water. However, after seven minutes and 12 seconds, he had to be pulled from the water because he was in trouble. He failed by one minute and 50 seconds.

REVOLUTION

In November 2006 David entered a large globe that was hung near Times Square in New York. He spent the next 52 hours without food or water while it turned eight times a minute before freeing himself and jumping down to the ground. To celebrate his success he took 100 poor children to a local store where they were each given $500 to spend.

ELECTRIFIED

In October 2012 David spent 72 hours on top of a pillar while more than one million volts of electricity were sent in his direction. He wore a special suit to protect him and make sure that none of the electricity entered his body. He didn't sleep or eat the whole time. The whole performance was filmed and shown live on YouTube.

3 Read the article again. Which event(s) …

1 lasted for more than five days?
_____

2 didn't end exactly as he had hoped it would?
_____

3 failed to impress some of the audience?
_____

4 saw him trapped in a ball?
_____

5 did he wear special clothing for?
_____

6 saw him not eat or drink water?
_____

4 Which of David's stunts would you be most scared to do? Write a short paragraph explaining why.

Pronunciation
The /ʒ/ phoneme
Go to page 119.

DEVELOPING WRITING

Describing a process

1 Read the text and match the words in the list with the pictures.

| 1 pulp | 2 wood fibers | 3 bark | 4 log | 5 branch | 6 roll of paper |

 A

 B

 C

 D

 E

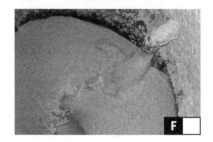 F

[1] We all know that paper comes from trees, but how exactly do you turn a solid piece of wood into the thin sheets of paper that we use every day?

[2] First of all, the trees are cut down. This means, of course, that every year millions of new trees need to be planted to make sure there will be enough trees for future paper production.

[3] When the tree has been cut down, the branches are taken off to make logs. The logs are loaded onto trucks and taken to the paper mill. At the paper mill, the logs are first put into a grinder machine where the outer layer of the tree, called the *bark*, is taken off. After that, they are put into another machine where they are compressed tightly and broken into tiny pieces called *fiber*. Next, water is added to the fiber to make a thick soup-like liquid called *pulp*.

[4] The pulp is then sprayed into very thin sheets in a paper-making machine. These sheets are passed under huge rollers that squeeze a lot of the water out. But the paper is still too wet, so it is passed under heated rollers to dry it out completely. Finally, the dry sheets of paper are rolled up, ready to be taken from the paper mill.

2 In which paragraph is …

1 the forest process described? ☐
2 the paper mill process described? ☐
3 the subject introduced? ☐
4 the final process described? ☐

3 Put the forest process in order. Then write the process in a short paragraph. Use *first, next, after that,* and *finally*.

In the forest

a ☐ Branches taken off
b ☐ Logs taken to paper mill
c ☐ Trees cut down
d ☐ Logs loaded onto trucks

4 Choose one of the processes below (or one of your own) and write a short text of about 200 words to describe it.

- How dried pasta is made
- How glass is made
- How ice cream is made
- How politicians are elected

CHECKLIST ✓

☐ Use words to describe a process
☐ Explain the process in order
☐ Explain how the process is finished

LISTENING

1 🔊24 **Put the instructions for the card trick in order. Then listen and check.**

How to amaze your friends with a card trick.

☐ **a** "I will now find your card from these ones on the table."

☐ **b** "Put your card on top of the bottom half of the deck."

☐ **c** "Choose any card from the deck. Don't tell me what it is."

☐ **d** "Is this your card?"

2 🔊24 **Listen again. Complete the sentences from the listening with the missing words.**

1 _____, ask your friend to choose a card and look at it secretly.

2 _____, cut the deck of cards into two halves.

3 _____ _____, ask your friend to put the card on the top of the bottom half of the deck.

4 _____, put the deck back together and go through the cards.

3 🔊25 **Listen and order the pictures.**

How to apply a decal (a fake tattoo).

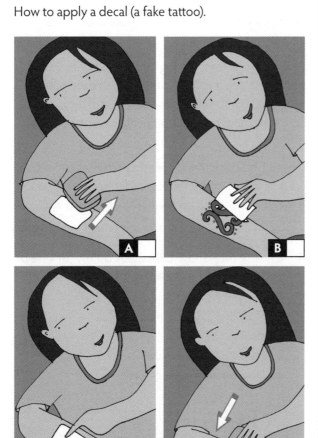

A ☐ B ☐ C ☐ D ☐

4 🔊25 **Listen again and complete the instructions.**

1 _____, put the decal face down on your arm or wherever you want to put it.

2 _____ put a wet sponge (but not too wet) on top and press hard.

3 _____ about a minute, take the sponge away.

4 _____, very slowly pull the transfer paper away. It should leave the decal on your skin.

DIALOGUE

1 **Put the dialogue in the correct order.**

a ☐ MAN — Three minutes? I'll remember that next time.

b ☐ MAN — For about five minutes.

c ☐ MAN — No, I didn't. I didn't know I had to.

d ☐ MAN — No, I didn't. I was way too hungry.

e ☐1 MAN — Oh dear. I've really messed up this egg. What did I do wrong?

f ☐ WOMAN — Finally, did you wait a minute before you started to eat it?

g ☐ WOMAN — That's the first thing you should always do. How long did you cook it?

h ☐ WOMAN — That's way too long. Three minutes is all you need.

i ☐ WOMAN — Did you wash the uncooked egg?

2 **Complete the conversation with the words in the list.**

now | first | then | finally | after | online

MILLIE Hi, Mom. Are you having trouble with something?

MOM Yes, I want to post this photograph ¹_____, but I don't know how to do it.

MILLIE OK, let me help you. ²_____, click here, where it says "photo/video."

MOM Ah, OK.

MILLIE ³_____ that, click on "upload photo." Great! ⁴_____ it's asking you which photo you want to upload.

MOM OK. I want this one here.

MILLIE OK, so just double-click on it. And ⁵_____ write something about the photo if you want.

MOM All right.

MILLIE And ⁶_____, click on "upload" and that's it! You're done!

Reading and Use of English part 5

You are going to read another excerpt from *The Mind Map*. For questions 1–4, choose the answer (A, B, C, or D) that you think fits best according to the text. Look back at the exam guide in Unit 5 on how to answer this question type.

The Mind Map by David Morrison

Eva was thinking hard. She looked past Lucho. He turned and saw that she was looking at a little yellow bird that had landed on the grass behind him.

"I've seen this bird a lot recently," he said. "Maybe it's trying to help me."

Eva corrected him, "Maybe it's trying to help us, Lucho."

Lucho smiled.

"Come on," he said. "Let's follow it."

Lucho pulled Eva up by the hand and they followed the little bird over the grass, toward the door to the school building. When they reached the door, Mr. Parra, the history teacher, was walking out of the building.

"How is your mind map going, you two?" Mr. Parra asked.

Lucho was not sure what to say. They couldn't tell Mr. Parra that the mind map seemed to be alive.

"It's going well, sir," said Eva, "but we have a question to ask you. Do you know what 'Ichua' means?"

Mr. Parra smiled.

"Ichua is the name of the most important place in the world for the Kogi," he explained. "Their most important chiefs are buried there. The Kogi say it is a secret underground place full of gold, but historians don't believe that it's a real place. I see you have spent your time well in the library."

It was Lucho's turn to ask a question. "Mr. Parra, do you know if there is a hotel in Santa Marta called the Hotel Continental?"

"Why?" Mr. Parra was laughing. "Are you planning a vacation?"

"No, sir," answered Lucho, feeling a little stupid.

"Well, there was a hotel called the Hotel Continental in Santa Marta, near the port. But it closed a few years ago," Mr. Parra explained.

Eva watched the little yellow bird fly up to the roof of the library.

"Any more questions?" Mr. Parra asked.

"Yes," said Eva. "Are birds important in Kogi stories?"

"Oh yes, Eva. There is a bird in every Kogi story. A bird brings a message to the jaguar or it helps the jaguar in its work. The jaguar, of course, is the most important animal for the Kogi and for many other tribes. The jaguar looks after the Kogi. Without the help of the jaguar, the Kogi believe, the sun would not rise, plants would not grow, and rain would not fall."

Mr. Parra smiled.

"I must say I am very pleased that you have been working so well. Don't forget to put all the information on your mind map and bring it to class on Monday."

Eva and Lucho watched Mr. Parra as he walked away from the school building. Lucho's head was full of questions. Had he dreamed that the mind map had grown? Had he added new words in his sleep? But then, why had the message "TAKE IT BACK" appeared on the computer screen and on Eva's cell phone? What did the pendant want? Did he have to take it back to Ichua? But how could he? Mr. Parra had said that Ichua probably wasn't a real place.

1   Eva corrects Lucho about the bird because …
    A   he doesn't know what kind of bird it is.
    B   she wants to let him know that she's decided to help him.
    C   he misunderstands how the bird is trying to help them.
    D   she thinks they should follow it.

2   Which of these statements is not true about Mr. Parra?
    A   He teaches history at the school.
    B   He gave Lucho and Eva the mind map homework.
    C   He is happy that the children are taking their homework seriously.
    D   He was walking in the same direction as the children when they met him.

3   What do we learn about the Kogi from their stories?
    A   They are the only tribe for whom the jaguar is an important animal.
    B   They like birds.
    C   They put jaguars in all their stories.
    D   Nature is very important to them.

4   What does the final paragraph suggest about Lucho?
    A   He thinks he might be doing things in his sleep.
    B   He wanted to ask Mr. Parra more questions.
    C   He's sure he's started to imagine things.
    D   He's really confused about the whole mind map mystery.

CONSOLIDATION

LISTENING

1 🔊 **26** **Listen and** (circle) **A, B, or C.**

1 How long did the story for homework have to be?
   A 50,000 words
   B 5,000 words
   C 500 words

2 What did the story have to be about?
   A ghosts
   B crime
   C romance

3 If the teacher likes his story, the boy might …
   A help the girl to write one.
   B send it to a website.
   C publish it in the school magazine.

2 🔊 **26** **Listen again and answer the questions.**

1 Why does the boy enjoy homework that involves writing a story?
   _____

2 How does he usually get an idea for a story?
   _____

3 How long did he spend writing the story?
   _____

4 Where did he get the idea for the story from?
   _____

5 What does the girl want the boy to do?
   _____

GRAMMAR

3 (Circle) **the correct options.**

1 There was an accident, and a lot of people *hurt / were hurt.*

2 These books *are written / were written* a very long time ago.

3 The new school *will be opened / will open* by the mayor tomorrow.

4 I don't understand computers, so I always *repair my computer / have my computer repaired* when there's a problem.

5 They *have built / have been built* a lot of new buildings here.

6 I went to the hairdresser's and *cut my hair / had my hair cut.*

7 Thirty people *have taken / have been taken* to the hospital.

8 Doctors *operate / are operated* on more than 30 people here every day.

4 **Complete the sentences with *who, whose, where, that,* or *which.***

1 That's the school _____ Dad taught.

2 Mr. Newson, my math teacher, is someone _____ I've learned a lot from.

3 I've forgotten _____ book this is.

4 Julian, _____ is a small town near Los Angeles, is where my sister lives.

5 Careful, it's the dog _____ tried to bite me.

6 Look, that's the guy _____ was on the news last night.

VOCABULARY

5 **Complete the words.**

1 I thought the play was a_____ fantastic.

2 Some of the things were so funny – in fact, they were h_____ .

3 One actor said something that didn't make s_____ to me, but it didn't matter.

4 One actor was very young, but she did very well. She was a_____ , in fact.

5 She played the part of the evil v_____ in the play.

6 We were all very happy that we had seen the play. In fact we were d_____ !

7 The theater was very big. I've never seen such an e_____ theater in my life!

8 It was a little noisy, so sometimes I couldn't hear the d_____ onstage very well.

6 **Complete the conversation with the words in the list.**

characters | crime | ending | hero | plot | setting | villain

STEVE I read a good book last week. It was called *Detective Grange Investigates.*

EMILY What's it about?

STEVE Well, it's a [1]_____ novel. The [2]_____ is Chicago at the end of the 19th century. And of course, the [3]_____ of the story is Detective Grange.

EMILY And what's the [4]_____ ?

STEVE Well, it's about how Grange finds out who stole some money from a rich family's house. Grange meets all kinds of different people – there are some funny [5]_____ and some horrible ones! The worst person is Dangerous Dan. He's the [6]_____ of the story. At the end …

EMILY No, no! Don't tell me the [7]_____ ! I might read the book myself!

DIALOGUE

7 **Complete the conversation with the phrases in the list. There are two extra phrases.**

it isn't strange | let me finish | the strangest thing happened | what are the chances
you'll never believe | what's strange | that's the annoying thing | I don't understand

JAKE   ¹_____ to me last weekend. I had a dream on Sunday about being lost in a completely empty city.

SUSIE   ²_____ about that? People have dreams all the time – including dreams about being lost.

JAKE   I know. But the next day on TV there was a movie where a woman was lost in an empty city, too. Just like my dream. ³_____ of that happening?

SUSIE   Well, not a lot, I suppose. But it's only a coincidence, isn't it?

JAKE   No, ⁴_____. There's more! You see, in the movie, when the woman was lost, she started to hear a loud noise, like a wild animal or something. And ⁵_____ what happened next! A tiger suddenly appeared in front of her! Now, in my dream, I started to hear a strange noise, too!

SUSIE   And did a tiger appear in your dream?

JAKE   Well, ⁶_____. You see, just when the noise started, I woke up! So I don't know if there was a tiger in my dream or not. But my cat was lying on my bed!

READING

8 **Read the book review and answer the questions.**

1 What kind of stories was Paul Auster looking for?
  A real stories that weren't too long
  B the listeners' favorite stories
  C true stories about famous people

2 Why did he decide to put the stories in the book?
  A because he wanted to share them all with the public
  B to make some money
  C because he couldn't read them all on the radio

3 What does the reviewer recommend?
  A to read the book from start to finish
  B to pick and choose stories from the book
  C to only read the sections you are most interested in

4 What is the reviewer's overall opinion of the book?
  A He liked it because the stories are so well written.
  B He liked it because some of the stories are very moving.
  C He liked another book of real-life stories more.

WRITING

9 **Write a brief review of a story that you like – perhaps from a movie, TV show, book, or even a true story about you or a friend. Write 150–200 words.**

Review:
True Tales of American Life

In 1999 the writer Paul Auster was asked if he would contribute stories to America's National Public Radio. But Auster decided to ask listeners to send in their stories instead. He wanted true stories that seemed like fiction. They could be about anything at all; they just had to be true and short. The ones chosen would be read aloud on the radio.

To Auster's surprise, more than 4,000 listeners sent in stories. It would have been impossible to read them all on the radio, so Auster took almost 200 of them and put them in a book – this book.

I liked some things about the collection, others not so much. Because the stories were written by ordinary people, they're not always well written. (I hate to think what the ones that weren't included were like!) And the categorization into sections like *Families*, *Objects*, *Strangers*, or *Animals* means that if you read one story after the other, it can be a little repetitive. But with any book of separate stories, you can just read one whenever you feel like it. You don't have to read it straight through, and that's probably the best thing to do here, too.

What's great about these stories is their veracity – they're all true, no matter how unbelievable (and some of them really are incredible). One or two of the stories were so painful they left me almost in tears.

So overall it's worth getting and reading. If you're into real-life stories like these, I'd also recommend a collection called *The Moth* … but more on that next time.

PRONUNCIATION

UNIT 1
Linking words with *up*

1 Match the sentence halves.

0 I find it difficult to get   `d`

1 I have too much homework. I spend ☐

2 Hi, Kelly! What's ☐

3 Now that it's winter, why don't you take ☐

4 Last night we stayed ☐

5 We'd like you to come, but it's ☐

6 Have you seen Jim? I wonder what he's ☐

7 She's 90 now and isn't ☐

8 I don't want to move. If it was ☐

9 The test has started. Please pick ☐

a up? You look really sad!

b up your pen and start writing.

c up to me, I'd stay here.

d up early.

e up to going for long walks.

f up skiing? It's so much fun!

g up to three hours a night doing it.

h up late talking about our vacation.

i up to these days.

j up to you.

2 🔊05 Listen, check, and repeat.

3 Write the phrases with *up* in the column that corresponds to the correct linked sound.

d sound	*get up*
k sound	
s sound	
z sound	

4 🔊06 Listen, check, and repeat.

UNIT 2
Initial consonant clusters with /s/

1 Complete the words with the correct letters. These are all /s/ consonant clusters.

0 I like the shirt that boy's wearing – the one with black and white ___*str*___ ipes.

1 A _____ong wind was blowing from the east.

2 The modern artist draws people as combinations of circles and _____ares.

3 They heard a loud _____ash as the rock fell into the river.

4 She had a headache from looking at the computer _____een all morning.

5 The fire _____ead quickly because of the heat and wind.

6 The people were _____eaming on the roller coaster ride.

2 🔊08 Listen, check, and repeat.

UNIT 3
Strong and weak forms: /ɑv/ and /əv/

1 Match the questions and answers.

0 What do you always buy the same brand **of**?   `c`

1 What are your favorite shoes made **of**? ☐

2 What kinds **of** clothes do you have the most **of**? ☐

3 Do you have a lot **of** gadgets? ☐

4 Which **of** your gadgets do you use the most? ☐

a My phone. Most **of** my friends have one, so we text each other a lot.

b They're made **of** leather, and they have rubber soles.

c Chocolate! I love the taste **of** Kalen's Chocolate Flowers.

d I'm a pretty casual person. I have a lot **of** jeans and T-shirts.

e Not really. Most **of** them, like the computer and game console, belong to my whole family.

2 🔊12 Listen and check.

3 Underline the weak forms and circle the strong forms of the word *of* in the sentences.

4 🔊12 Listen again, check, and repeat.

UNIT 4
Consonant–vowel word linking

1 Underline the words where the final consonant is linked to the vowel sound in the next word.

0 I like that movie. It's about two friends who go traveling.

1 I didn't find out who wrote the message.

2 My dad doesn't walk to work anymore.

3 Her family lived in Paris before they came to Seattle.

4 They lost everything when their house burned down.

5 Jenny's mom gets angry when she doesn't clean up her room.

6 Can we have a break now?

7 It was so difficult to make up my mind!

8 Tom worked out the solution to the math problem in less than a minute!

9 The climb was difficult, so she gave up before she got to the top.

2 🔊17 **Listen, check, and repeat.**

3 Write the phrases with the linked sound in the correct column.

t sound	d sound	k sound	s sound	v sound
			it's about	

4 🔊18 **Listen, check, and repeat.**

UNIT 5
/ə/ in word endings

1 Complete the words with the correct spelling.

-on (x1) | -ent (x3) | -ion (x5) | -ate (x2)
-ous (x3) | -an (x1) | -al (x3) | -el (x1) | -es (x1)

0 The story will capture your attent _ion_ and imaginat _ion_ .

1 It's a historic_____ nov_____ about a desper_____ and danger_____ man.

2 Many fam_____ people live in centr_____ Lond_____.

3 The hospit_____ provided informat_____ about the accid_____.

4 The organizat_____ was confid_____ about the immedi_____ need for a new divis_____ in Los Angel_____.

5 That wom_____ is the obvi_____ choice for presid_____.

2 🔊21 **Listen, check, and repeat.**

UNIT 6
The /ʒ/ phoneme

1 🔊22 **Listen and circle the one word in each group that doesn't have the /ʒ/ phoneme.**

0	A casual	B usually	C revision	D caution
1	A sabotage	B version	C engine	D camouflage
2	A Asia	B Russia	C treasure	D collision
3	A magician	B illusionist	C occasion	D explosion
4	A pleasure	B television	C pleasant	D decision
5	A confusion	B revision	C measure	D permission
6	A unusual	B mansion	C vision	D leisure
7	A exposure	B usual	C fashion	D diversion
8	A erosion	B decoration	C illusion	D invasion

(D caution is circled)

2 🔊22 **Listen again, check, and repeat.**

3 Complete the sentences with the words in the list.

Asia | casual | pleasure | decision | illusionist
occasion | collision | version | ~~usually~~

0 I don't _usually_ have to study more than an hour on the weekend.

1 A Thank you for helping me today.
  B It was my _____ .

2 There was a terrible _____ on the highway today, but no one was hurt.

3 Dynamo is an amazing _____ .

4 I'm saving this beautiful dress to wear for a special _____ .

5 I liked that movie, but I prefer the original _____ .

6 I've always wanted to travel around _____ .

7 It wasn't an easy _____ , but I finally chose a career in biology.

8 She prefers _____ clothes and wears jeans and T-shirts most of the time.

4 🔊23 **Listen, check, and repeat.**

GRAMMAR REFERENCE

UNIT 1
Present tenses (review)

To talk about the present, we mostly use the following tenses: simple present, present continuous, present perfect, and present perfect continuous

1 We use the simple present to talk about facts and give opinions and to talk about regular habits.

   It **takes** around four minutes to boil an egg. (fact)
   I **think** this is awful. (opinion)
   I usually **go** to bed around eleven o'clock. (habit)

2 We use the present continuous to talk about what's happening at or around the time of speaking.

   What **are** you **doing**?
   A TV company **is making** a show about life plans.

3 We use the present perfect to talk about past actions and experiences but without saying exactly when. This tense links the present and the past, and we often use it when a past event has an effect on the present.

   She**'s read** lots of articles about this, and she**'s learned** a lot.
   The storm **has caused** a lot of flooding in the town.

4 We use the present perfect continuous to talk about actions that started in the past and are still happening.

   I**'ve been trying** to get in shape for several weeks now.

Future tenses (review)

To talk about the future, we mostly use the following tenses: present continuous, will / won't (do), and going to (do)

1 We often use the present continuous to talk about future plans and arrangements.

   I**'m taking** a guitar lesson tomorrow morning.

2 We often use will / won't (do) to make predictions.

   She's very smart. I'm sure she**'ll do** really well in college.
   This is the dry time of year; it **won't rain** again until September.

3 We often use going to (do) to talk about intentions.

   Next year, I**'m going to start** college.
   Where **are** you **going to** go on vacation next year?

UNIT 2
Narrative tenses (review)

To talk about the past and to tell narratives, we mostly use the following tenses: simple past, past continuous, and past perfect

1 We use the simple past to talk about actions that happened at one moment in the past or were true at one time in the past.

   I **fell** down.
   People **didn't have** easy lives 200 years ago.

2 We use the past continuous to describe ongoing actions or situations around a time in the past.

   I **was running** really fast (and I fell down).
   Thousands of people **were living** in enclosed spaces.

   We also use the past continuous to talk about an ongoing action that was interrupted by another.

   The fire started while people **were sleeping**.

3 We use the past perfect to describe an event that happened before another.

   The weather **had been** very hot when the fire broke out.
   When we arrived the movie **had** already **started**.

UNIT 3
(don't) have to / ought to / should(n't) / must

1 We use have to to say "this is important or necessary." We use must to say that we, or other people, have an obligation to do something.

   Our train leaves at seven o'clock, so I **have to get up** early.
   I **must save** some money for Mom's birthday present.
   You **must try** to work harder, Jack.

2 We use don't have to to say "this is NOT important or necessary."

   You **don't have to come** with us if you don't want to.

3 We use *should* or *ought to* to tell someone that something is a good idea.

*At the beach, you **should wear** sunscreen.*
*That wasn't a nice thing to say; you **ought to** apologize.*

Remember: *ought to* isn't as frequent as *should*. It is used mostly in writing, and the negative form is rare.

4 We use *shouldn't* to tell someone that something is not a good idea.

*You **shouldn't spend** so much money on clothes.*

had ('d) better (not)

We use *had / 'd better (not)* to advise or warn people in strong terms. It is used to tell people about negative results in the future if they do / don't do something.

The form is always past (*had*), and it is often shortened to *'d*.

*You**'d better** hurry up (or you'll miss the train).*
*He**'d better not** say that again (or I will be very angry).*

can('t) / must (not)

1 When we want to talk or ask about permission, we often use the modal verb *can / can't*.

*You **can go** to the party, but you **can't stay** late.*
***Can** I **borrow** your phone to make a call?*

2 To say what isn't allowed, we use *can't* or *must not*.

*You **can't park** here. (This is a fact / rule.)*
*You **must not leave** your things on the floor! (The speaker isn't allowing something.)*

UNIT 4
First and second conditional (review)

1 We use the first conditional to talk about real situations and their consequences. It consists of two clauses. The *if* + simple present clause introduces the possible situation or condition. The *will / won't* clause gives the result or consequence.

*If you **leave** that door open, the cat **will get** out.*
*If we **don't leave** now, we **won't get** to school on time.*

2 We use the second conditional to talk about hypothetical or very unlikely situations and their (imaginary) consequences. It consists of two clauses. The *if* + simple past clause introduces the hypothetical situation. The *would* clause gives the imagined result or consequence.

*If I **had** a cat, I**'d call** it Max. (I don't have a cat.)*
*If we **didn't have** a cat, we **wouldn't have to** spend money on cat food. (We have a cat, and we need to spend money on cat food.)*

Time conjunctions

We can join ideas about future actions or situations using words like: *if, unless, until, when, as soon as*

When we use these words, we use them with the simple present tense (not *will / won't*) even though the clause refers to the future.

*She won't be happy **if** you **forget** her birthday.*
*We'll be late **unless** we **leave** now.*
*I won't stop asking you **until** you **tell** me.*
*They'll be hungry **when** they **get** here.*
*I'll call you **as soon as** I **finish** this work.*

wish and if only

1 We use *wish* or *if only* + simple past to say that we would like a present situation to be different from what it actually is.

*I **wish** I **had** more friends. (I don't have many friends.)*
*My friends **wish** they **were** rich. (They aren't rich.)*

2 We use *wish / if only* + *could* to talk about wanting to have the ability or permission to do something.

*I **wish** I **could** speak Italian.*
***If only** you **could** come with me.*

3 If there is a situation we don't like (for example, someone is doing or always does something that annoys us), we can use *wish / if only* + *would(n't)*.

*I **wish** you **would knock** before coming into my room.*
***If only** he **wouldn't talk** about soccer all the time!*

Third conditional

We use the third conditional to talk about how things might have been different in the past. The third conditional is formed with *If* + past perfect + *would (not) have* + past participle. The third conditional talks about impossible conditions (because the past cannot be changed).

*If I**'d been** careful, I **wouldn't have dropped** the camera. (I wasn't careful, so I dropped the camera.)*
*If you **hadn't woken** me up, I **would have slept** for hours. (You woke me up so I didn't sleep for hours.)*

UNIT 5
Relative pronouns

We use relative pronouns to start a relative clause.

1 To refer to people, we use *who* or *that*.

He's a writer. He wrote that fantastic story.
→ *He's the writer **who** / **that** wrote that fantastic story.*

2 To refer to things, we use *which* or *that*.

It's a great story. It was made into a movie.
→ *It's a great story, **which** was also made into a movie.*
→ *It's a great story **that** was made into a great movie.*

3 To refer to possessions, we use *whose*.

I know a boy. His sister is on TV.
→ *I know a boy **whose** sister is on TV.*

4 To refer to places, we use *where*.

This is the town. I was born here.
→ *This is the town **where** I was born.*

Defining and non-defining relative clauses

There are two kinds of relative clause: <u>defining</u> and <u>non-defining</u>.

1 A defining relative clause identifies an object, a person, a place, or a possession. We need this information to know who or what is being talked about. When we write these sentences, we don't use any commas.

The woman was a genius. She wrote this book.
→ *The woman **who wrote this book** was a genius.*
I saw a movie last night. The movie was terrible.
→ *The movie **that I saw last night** was terrible.*

2 We use non-defining relative clauses to add extra information, which is not needed to understand the sentence. We put commas around these clauses when we write them. They are rarely used in conversational language.

My uncle lives in Sydney. He's a successful writer.
→ *My uncle, **who lives in Sydney**, is a successful writer.*

Relative clauses with *which*

1 When we want to refer back to a whole idea or clause, we use the relative pronoun *which*.

He went into the desert alone. It was a dangerous thing to do.
→ *He went into the desert alone, **which** was a dangerous thing to do.*

2 We cannot use *that* or *what* in this way – only *which*.

*Stephen King has sold millions of books, **which** (~~that~~ / ~~what~~) has made him very rich.*

UNIT 6
Present and past passive (review)

1 We use the passive (present or past) to say what happens or happened to the subject of the sentence. Often the cause of the action is unknown or unimportant.

2 We form the passive with a form of the verb *be* and the past participle of the verb.

*English and French **are spoken** in Canada.*
*The roof of the house **was destroyed** in the storm.*

3 We use the preposition *by* to say who or what does the action, but only if this is important.

My bike was stolen. (We don't know, or it isn't important, who stole it.)
*The magic show was watched **by** more than 500 people. (It's important to say how many people watched the show.)*

have something done

1 We use the structure *have something done* when we talk about someone else doing a function or service for us.

*My grandma's very old so she has **her meals cooked** for her. (Another person cooks her meals for her.)*
*They **had their car repaired**. (They paid a mechanic to repair their car.)*

2 It is formed with *have* + noun + past participle.

*I **had my phone repaired** last week.*

3 In less formal contexts, *get* often replaces *have*.

*I'm going to **get my hair done** for the party tonight.*

Future and present perfect passive

1 The future passive is formed with *will be / won't be* + past participle.

*The new supermarket **will be opened** next week by a famous TV actor.*

2 The present perfect passive is formed with *have / has (not) been* + past participle.

*The streets of our town look awful. They **haven't been cleaned** for two weeks.*

IRREGULAR VERBS

Base form	Past simple	Past participle
be	was / were	been
beat	beat	beaten
become	became	become
begin	began	begun
bite	bit	bitten
blow	blew	blown
break	broke	broken
breed	bred	bred
bring	brought	brought
build	built	built
buy	bought	bought
can	could	–
catch	caught	caught
choose	chose	chosen
come	came	come
cost	cost	cost
cut	cut	cut
do	did	done
draw	drew	drawn
dream	dreamed	dreamed
drink	drank	drunk
drive	drove	driven
eat	ate	eaten
fall	fell	fallen
feel	felt	felt
fight	fought	fought
find	found	found
flee	fled	fled
fly	flew	flown
forget	forgot	forgotten
forgive	forgave	forgiven
freeze	froze	frozen
get	got	gotten
give	gave	given
go	went	gone
grow	grew	grown
hang	hung	hung
have	had	had
hear	heard	heard
hide	hid	hidden
hit	hit	hit
hold	held	held
hurt	hurt	hurt
keep	kept	kept
know	knew	known
lay	laid	laid
lead	led	led
learn	learned	learned
leave	left	left

Base form	Past simple	Past participle
lend	lent	lent
let	let	let
lie	lay	lain
light	lit	lit
lose	lost	lost
make	made	made
mean	meant	meant
meet	met	met
pay	paid	paid
put	put	put
quit	quit	quit
read	read	read
ride	rode	ridden
ring	rang	rung
rise	rose	risen
run	ran	run
say	said	said
see	saw	seen
seek	sought	sought
sell	sold	sold
send	sent	sent
set	set	set
shake	shook	shaken
shoot	shot	shot
show	showed	shown
shut	shut	shut
sing	sang	sung
sink	sank	sunk
sit	sat	sat
sleep	slept	slept
speak	spoke	spoken
spend	spent	spent
spill	spilled	spilled
spread	spread	spread
stand	stood	stood
steal	stole	stolen
stick	stuck	stuck
strike	struck	struck
swim	swam	swum
swing	swung	swung
take	took	taken
teach	taught	taught
tell	told	told
think	thought	thought
throw	threw	thrown
understand	understood	understood
wake	woke	woken
wear	wore	worn
win	won	won
write	wrote	written

Acknowledgements

The authors and publishers acknowledge the following sources of copyright material and are grateful for the permissions granted. While every effort has been made, it has not always been possible to identify the sources of all the material used or to trace all copyright holders. If any omissions are brought to our notice, we will be happy to include the appropriate acknowledgements on reprinting.

Cambridge University Press for the text on p. 61 from "The Mind Map Level 3 Lower-intermediate" by David Morrison. Copyright © 2009 by Cambridge University Press. Reproduced with permission of Cambridge University Press;

Experience project for the text on p. 76 from "I Got Caught Shoplifting." Copyright by Experience project. Reproduced with permission of Experience project;

Random History for the text on p. 94 from "99 Valuable Facts About," 2013. Copyright © 2013 by Random History. Reproduced with permission of Random History;

Cambridge University Press for the text on p. 115 from "Bullring Kid and Country Cowboy Level 4 Intermediate" by Louise Clover, 2010. Copyright © 2010 by Cambridge University Press. Reproduced with permission of Cambridge University Press.

Corpus
Development of this publication has made use of the Cambridge English Corpus (CEC). The CEC is a computer database of contemporary spoken and written English, which currently stands at over one billion words. It includes British English, American English, and other varieties of English. It also includes the Cambridge Learner Corpus, developed in collaboration with Cambridge English Language Assessment. Cambridge University Press has built up the CEC to provide evidence about language use that helps to produce better language teaching materials.

English Profile
This product is informed by the English Vocabulary Profile, built as part of English Profile, a collaborative program designed to enhance the learning, teaching, and assessment of English worldwide. Its main funding partners are Cambridge University Press and Cambridge English Language Assessment, and its aim is to create a "profile" for English linked to the Common European Framework of Reference for Languages (CEF). English Profile outcomes, such as the English Vocabulary Profile, will provide detailed information about the language that learners can be expected to demonstrate at each CEF level, offering a clear benchmark for learners' proficiency. For more information, please visit www.englishprofile.org

Cambridge Dictionaries
Cambridge dictionaries are the world's most widely used dictionaries for learners of English. The dictionaries are available in print and online at dictionary.cambridge.org. Copyright © Cambridge University Press, reproduced with permission.

The authors and publishers acknowledge the following sources of copyright material and are grateful for the permissions granted. While every effort has been made, it has not always been possible to identify the sources of all the material used, or to trace all copyright holders. If any omissions are brought to our notice, we will be happy to include the appropriate acknowledgements on reprinting and in the next update to the digital edition, as applicable.

The publishers are grateful to the following for permission to reproduce copyright photographs and material:

Key: L = Left, C = Center, R = Right, T = Top, B = Below, B/G = Background

p. 4: ©Hill Street Studios/Blend Images/Getty Images; p. 6: ©Goodluz/ Shutterstock; p. 14: ©karelnoppe/Shutterstock; p. 15: ©Monkey Business Images/Shutterstock; p. 19: ©Monkey Business Images/Shutterstock; p. 22: ©The Art Archive/Alamy; p. 24: ©VisitBritain/Britain On View/Getty Images; p. 27: Charles Dickens at the Blacking Factory, an illustration from 'The Leisure Hour', 1904 (engraving), Barnard, Frederick (1846-96) (after)/Private Collection/Bridgeman Images; p. 29 (TL): ©Becky Stares/Shutterstock; p. 29 (TR): ©Arcady/Shutterstock; p. 29 (CL): ©Vitezslav Valka/Shutterstock; p. 29 (CR): ©konstantinks/Shutterstock; p. 29 (BL, BR): ©Arcady/Shutterstock; p. 32: ©Fuse/Getty Images; p. 40: ©ITV/REX; p. 48: ©KIM NGUYEN/Shutterstock; p. 50: ©Lebrecht Music and Arts Photo Library/Alamy; p. 51: 'The Boy Who Biked the World' 'On the Road to Africa' (part 1) (Nov 2011). Published by Eye Books. Used with permission; p. 58: ©Bobby Bank/WireImage/Getty Images; p. 59 (TL): ©sauletas/Shutterstock; p. 59 (TC): ©Neirfy/Shutterstock; p. 59 (TR): ©Ryan DeBerardinis/Shutterstock; p. 59 (BL): ©Vladimir Caplinskij/Shutterstock; p. 59 (BC): ©SUSUMU NISHINAGA/SCIENCE PHOTO LIBRARY; p. 59 (BR): ©Lourens Smak/Alamy

Cover photographs by: (TR): ©Stephen Moore/Digital Vision Vectors/Getty Images; (L): ©Andrea Haase/iStock/Getty Images Plus/Getty Images; (BR): ©Pete Starman/Stone/Getty Images.

The publishers are grateful to the following illustrators:
Bryan Beach (Advocate Art) 34
David Semple 7, 28, 39, 42, 57
Fred van Deelen (The Organisation) 20
Julian Mosedale 11, 36, 55, 60

The publishers are grateful to the following contributors:
Blooberry: text design and layouts; Claire Parson: cover design; Hilary Fletcher: picture research; CityVox: audio recordings; Karen Elliott: Pronunciation sections; Matt Norton: Get it right! exercises